KING GEORGE VI

GEORGE VI

King George VI

An Intimate and Authoritative Life of the King by one who has had special facilities, and first published with the approval of His Majesty when Duke of York

By

TAYLOR DARBYSHIRE

HUTCHINSON & CO.

(Publishers) Ltd.

LONDON

Made and Printed in Great Britain at
The Mayflower Press, Plymouth. William Brendon & Son, Ltd.
1937

CONTENTS

LIST OF ILLUSTRATIONS

7

LIST OF ILLUSTRATIONS

KING GEORGE VI

CHAPTER ONE

EARLY CHILDHOOD

IT is generally understood that the two Royal Princesses, Elizabeth and Margaret Rose, the most widely adored children in the world, consider their father a most excellent playmate, with perhaps a tendency to romp. If that popular impression is correct, then it only goes to show the lasting benefit of early training. The three eldest children of King George V and Queen Mary were all born within three years of each other, were brought up through the nursery years together, and being all three of the right type of high-spirited English youth, they indulged themselves with every possible form of youthful high spirits. Therefore, remembering his own childhood, His Majesty the King can help his daughters to appreciate theirs. Tales of what happened when the Duke of Windsor, Prince Albert, as King George VI then was, and Princess Mary really laid themselves out for practical joking are still extant in the Royal households, and it is highly probable that the young princesses themselves have already heard some of them—and maybe profited by them.

Albert Frederick Arthur George was born at York Cottage, Sandringham, on December 14th, 1895, a few days less than eighteen months after his brother, Edward, and sixteen months before his sister, Princess Mary. "The parents young, the children small," is an oft-quoted French ideal of human happiness—and that ideal must have been realized in those last years of the old and first of the new century at Sandringham, at Marlborough House and wherever the Royal Family were. Life flowed on peacefully in the ordered routine of an English family—to be broken by the visits of the late King George V and Queen Mary, as the Duke and Duchess of Cornwall and York, to the Australian Commonwealth on the occasion of its inauguration and by other journeys undertaken in the fulfilment of the Royal Duties.

Until the Australian visit, the two Princes and their sister spent their time in the nursery and in the nursery schoolroom. In charge of the nursery was the much-loved " Mrs. Bill," a devoted member of the Royal staff whose years of service culminated when she retired full of honour from the post of housekeeper at Buckingham Palace to a well-earned rest. Her charges never forgot her, and in their turn their children were petted and spoilt as their father and mother had been. The nursery Governess was Madame Bricka, who had been for many years companion and Governess to Queen Mary.

On the return of the Duke and Duchess of Cornwall and York from Australia, the problem of training and teaching the young Princes was immediately taken up by their father and grandfather. Together they worked out a scheme for fitting the then Prince of Wales and Prince Albert to the duties they should one day assume as representatives of an Empire greater than any the world had seen. A fact not always remembered is the point that King Edward VII was the first really " British " King to ascend the throne—British in the sense that England, Ireland, Scotland, and Wales were united under one sovereign who had no continental territory. When Queen Victoria came to the throne in 1837, the English monarch ceased to be also King of Hanover, that title passing to her brother the Duke of Cumberland, and though the family name of Guelph was preserved until the great war, the British character of the House of Windsor was by that chance confirmed and when King Edward was crowned there was no longer any continental preoccupation in the hearts of the British Royal Family. King Edward himself had seen to it that his son was brought up in all the traditions of an English gentleman. Grandfather and father alike were determined that the third generation should profit by that same wonderful training.

For the boys' tutor, the choice fell on the late

Mr. H. P. Hansell, whose tall slim form and keen intellectual face were for many years seen at Buckingham Palace in his capacity of Gentleman Usher to King George, a post that fell to him as the reward of many years' earnest zeal in the teaching of all the King's sons in turn. He was a Malvern College and Magdalen, Oxford man and had gained experience in the handling of boys as a master at Rossall, a public school, and Ludgrove, a private school founded by A. T. B. Dunn, whose boys for the most part went to Eton. Mr. Hansell had specialized in holiday work, and from 1898 to 1901 had been a private tutor to Prince Arthur of Connaught. For a time, Madame Bricka helped with the French lessons, but during the tour of the Duke and Duchess of York in Australia they had met and been much impressed by Mademoiselle José Dussau, the French governess to the three sons of the late Lord Tennyson, then Governor of South Australia. Queen Mary made up her mind that she should eventually come to the Royal Children, and it was with very great reluctance that Lady Tennyson released her. She was appointed governess to Princess Mary in 1904 and took her place on the scholastic staff, as an added teacher to M. Hua, who had been appointed to the dual position of Librarian and French tutor to the Princes in May 1903. He had been French tutor to the Duke of Clarence and King George when the two brothers were in *Britannia* together, and subsequently had been a French master at Eton for eighteen years. With Mlle Dussau and M. Hua, French became a very thoroughly taught subject, and at meal-times in particular was invariably the conversational medium. The combination lasted until 1909—the year the King went to Osborne, when M. Hua died and Mlle Dussau carried on alone. While in London Mr. Hansell also had the assistance of Mr. M. S. David, a mathematical master from Tonbridge School.

So much for the educational side. But of almost as much importance were the physical and sporting side, and in those categories nothing was left undone to create the old classic ideal of " mens sana in corpore sano." As soon as they could stand at attention, drill, and military drill at that, commenced, first under the orders of Sergt.-Major Wright of the Coldstream Guards, who was later to become Mayor of Windsor, then under the instruction of Pipe-Major Henry Forsyth, Scots Guards, and Simon Cameron, once a private in the Cameron High-landers. While in London the social amenities were attended to with a dancing class at Marlborough House, though it is to be feared that the measures then taught are now no use in the modern ballroom. The late Mr. Cecil Sharp, who fought so hard for the revival and preservation of Folk Songs, had the children in a singing class, and as exercise in London was harder to come by than in the country, the Princes became, thus early, members of the Bath Club. It was then, and has remained until this day, a very happy playground for them. There they learnt to

swim and to play squash racquets, a game the love
of which has stayed with the King and the Duke of
Windsor, both, all through their lives. When the
Duke of Windsor began his tours of the Empire he
had a special racquet court built which he carried
on the deck of the battle-cruisers which took him to
the distant parts of the earth. That same court, a
little battered and the worse for wear but still quite
adequate for its purpose, was bought from his
brother by His Majesty, when he undertook his
world voyage in H.M.S. *Renown* in 1927. There
all through the tropics, sometimes in stifling heat
and always in a zinc-lined room that might have
been a bear pit, he played with one or other of the
officers of *Renown* or of his staff, a stiff game in the
afternoons.

It was, however, in the country and at the seaside
that His Majesty the King found his full delight in
those days. There all the sports that a healthy boy
delights in could be followed in turn as the round of
the seasons allowed. At Sandringham, the young
Princes played football with the village boys, and
gradually under the guidance of J. Walter Jones, the
local schoolmaster, a team was formed of calibre
good enough to play private school teams from
Hunstanton and elsewhere. As for the other
national game, cricket was played on the Royal
Household Ground at Frogmore with teams from
Eton and St. George's, Windsor, schools, during the
summer months. There is a story that the King
once performed that enviable feat, the hat trick,

his grandfather, father, and his uncle being the victims. His Majesty was coached in golf whenever there was a course available. At Windsor, Sandringham, and Balmoral, keepers, stalkers, and ghillies were all keen that the "young masters" should be as good shots and fishermen as their father, and never an opportunity was lost of teaching them the hunting craft in all its manifestations. Riding of course was an early accomplishment, and Mr. Stratton, who from the first was in charge, must have been a very proud man when shortly after the war the four Princes and Princess Mary all attended a meet of the West Norfolk Foxhounds.

It was a quiet and for the most part an uneventful time, those few years that elapsed from 1895 to 1909, when schooldays were left behind. His Majesty was too young to be affected by the Boer war, though the fortunes of the British armies in the field were followed by him and his brothers with boyish enthusiasm. Too young also to feel very keenly the death of his great-grandmother Queen Victoria, whom he scarcely remembers, though often during the first years of his life grandchildren and great-grandchildren were gathered under the same roof as the great Queen Empress. The year went by in its appointed course. The season was spent in London, first at York House and then at Marlborough House, with breaks of a few days or weeks at Frogmore, near Windsor Castle. In the late summer and early autumn the Family went to Abergeldie Castle, near Balmoral, and in the late autumn they went south to York Cottage at Sandringham, where with a fortnight at Windsor in January they stayed through the winter and spring until the season opened in London again. Perfectly normal procedure, perfectly planned to get the best results out of life and instil the best ideals into young brains eagerly alert to assimilate it all.

These years had one outstanding characteristic, aptly summed up by Mr. Hansell as " the shadow of the great house." As soon as King Edward ascended the throne and his son, the late King George V, became Prince of Wales, the home of the latter was never far away from where the Court happened to be. If at Buckingham Palace, then the Prince and Princess of Wales were at Marlborough House; if at Sandringham, then the Prince was at York Cottage; if at Windsor Castle, the Prince of Wales was at Frogmore. For Balmoral, Abergeldie Castle served as the home of the latter. So that His Majesty, as were his brothers, was always in touch with King Edward and Queen Alexandra. King Edward VII had in him from the birth of his first grandchild the determination that they should grow up in every way worthy of their great heritage, and all discipline, all contact, was directed to that end. Those early years of association with King Edward must have gone far towards the moulding of the character of the King and imbued him deeply with the determination we see to-day so manifest

Central News

H.M. THE KING AND THE DUKE OF WINDSOR (*left*) WITH
THEIR TUTOR, THE LATE MR. H. P. HANSELL

THE FOUR YOUNG PRINCES AT BALMORAL

Left to right. Prince George, Prince Albert, Prince Henry, the Prince of Wales

in him that whatever it be the "job" must be done and done faithfully and well. That is not to say that King Edward and Queen Alexandra were not indulgent grandparents—they most certainly were. While their father and mother were away on their Empire tour they superintended the care of the young family, and when the family was reunited it was the regular custom that the young Princes and Princess Mary should go up every evening to the Palace or Castle where King Edward was staying. It was then that most of the pranks and practical jokes of which the stories are now told had their origin. They were allowed to run wild through the rooms and corridors in a play hour in which King Edward took as much pleasure as his grandchildren. Indeed so uproarious was the fun sometimes that their mother, anxious for the behaviour of her children, felt that perhaps a check should now and again be placed on their high spirits. So Mr. Hansell was "told off" to accompany them in their visits. It was not a particularly grateful part to have to play, but the boys took it in good part, and if they evaded—as they did—the supervision of their tutor, the tutor did not tell.

CHAPTER TWO

FIRST YEARS IN THE NAVY

" LIFE," the real serious business of life, begins early for those destined for a career in the Navy, as the King was. For the first thirteen years of his existence he had tasted only the ordinary peaceful days that a well-bred English boy enjoys. A nursery with devoted staff, the healthful atmosphere of a private preparatory school as Mr. Hansell strove to reproduce it, changed when he had barely passed his fourteenth birthday to the barrack room—or one would say the warship " flat "—surroundings of the Naval Training College at Osborne. There was to be no molly-coddling. The King, or Prince Albert, went in as an ordinary cadet, with no privileges and no " marks of rank." To borrow an Americanism, he was " one of the class of 1909 " and was expected to behave exactly as every other boy in that class or any class was expected to behave. The system and the discipline which runs from end to end of the Navy begins early, and by slow degrees the cadet is taught to assume responsibility, to cultivate the habit of command, to practise diligence and self-control, to take all the kicks and none of the ha'pence, and above all to obey all orders " on the run," whether they came from the Admiral of the Fleet or from the senior cadet who had just hoisted his newly awarded badge. Nearly forty years ago Rudyard Kipling wrote thus of the Midshipman :

" For seven years, counting his time in the *Britannia*, he dresses at a chest and sleeps in a hammock, getting to know himself and his associates with that deadly stark intimacy that only flourishes in the Navy. There are no excuses in his Service. He must not answer back ; he must do as he is told—not immediately but sooner, much sooner. These are the years that weed out those who have mistaken their calling. The incompetents go home, and curse the Navy evermore. The virtuous stay on and learn to steal brass boiler tubes for their boats ; learn to smoke secretly in the fighting tops (they are forbidden tobacco till they are eighteen), fall into and out of all manner of tight places that require dexterity and a cheek of cold drawn brass ; pick up more than they learn under the Instructor from the talk of Warrant Officers and men and the carefully watched mistakes of their elders ; and when they reach commissioned rank impart their lore to their successors with a dirk scabbard."

It was into that environment the King entered as his father had done before him. The Navy does not change, at least in its essentials, and the same conditions applied to King George as to his son and as they apply to-day to the youngster just entering. It was in that environment that the King was to spend the next seven years of his life, gladly and eagerly looking forward always to the sea-going career he coveted so much and of which he was to be so unkindly cheated. From January 1909 to the end of 1917, his main ambition was to be a thoroughly efficient Naval officer. To that ambition he bent all his energies from the day he entered Osborne. Severe and recurrent attacks of a grave illness balked him in the end, and indeed all the time he was working his way up the service he had to fight this disadvantage only to have it conquer at last.

For the two years he spent at Osborne and the succeeding two years at Dartmouth the curriculum was a varied one. It included mathematics, physics, electricity, the science and practice of engineering, French, English composition and Literature, General Naval History, Navigation, and the Elements of Seamanship. It was in the last named that the naval training had varied most since the days of Nelson and into the middle of the nineteenth century. Until then the training of a Naval officer was almost entirely devoted to " ship handling " in all its branches. The youngsters were taught first and foremost to " Hand reef and steer," and at sea they spent almost as much time aloft as on deck. But when the

King entered Osborne, a fighting ship had already become an engine-room packed from bow to stern with all manner of mechanical devices to carry out by steam or electricity what once there had been only man power to accomplish. So we find that in the allocation of times in the study schedule engineering subjects claim a higher percentage than seamanship—the proportion being 30 to 20 per cent ; general subjects as enumerated occupying the balance. This division of interest between seamanship and engineering has had its reaction to-day with the King. He was a deeply interested student of both, and if anything his favourite subject was seamanship. Early on he could handle a boat better than most of his year, and it is on record that he was very scornful of the efforts in the same direction of his brother, the then Prince of Wales, who was of course at Osborne and Dart- mouth ahead of him,—as scornful that is as a younger brother can dare to be towards an elder or a junior cadet to a senior. But it was his engineering studies which were to be of most use to him in after years, and there is no doubt that the knowledge he gained, as Naval cadet and officer, of the science and practice of Engineering has stood and is standing him in good stead in his many visits to industrial centres and to factories to-day. It has enabled him to grasp quickly and thoroughly the very varying conditions and complicated machinery which he meets in his inspections, while no doubt the thoroughness that was required of him as a boy in his training gives him an added equipment in the searching questions he puts to factory superintendents when he goes his round.

The record of the King at Osborne and Dartmouth according to all, both tutors and class-mates, was an enviable one. A thorough good sort, anxious to work, still more anxious to play. He took the usual routine throughout and examinations found him " usually at the bottom of his lists "— says the King himself. Quiet, unassuming, and diffident of ever pushing himself forward, everybody liked him and admired his character. To that Captain W. D. Phipps, R.N., his term Lieutenant at Osborne, who retired from the Navy in 1920, bears enthusiastic tribute. There are two others who join in that commendation—the Rev. E. H. Arkwright, now vicar of Hollingbourne, Kent, who was his special tutor at Dartmouth, and Mr. J. Watt who held the same office at Osborne, where he was second master. There is a pretty little story to be told anent Mr. Watt. At the end of one summer term, the King went down with whooping-cough and spent the whole of the summer leave recuperating at Altnaguibsaigh, on Loch Muick, near Balmoral, with Mr. Watt in charge. The latter was a fine fisherman and taught the King the more delicate touches that distinguish the elect among fly-fishers from the ordinary water flogger. That was the sort of thing the King never forgot. When he was in New Zealand he heard that Mr. Watt was there also, on a visit to relatives. Though in the midst of a most strenuous tour when every minute that was not taken up with official duties was precious, he took an hour or two of his scanty leisure and motored several miles to see his old tutor and fight their battles o'er again.

In games no less than in the classroom, the King was emphatically one of the crowd. As already mentioned he was fondest of boat-sailing, though that came more perhaps into the category of training than sport. But on the playing field he was always keen. Playing a good game of football and taking the rough with the smooth with a cheerful imperturbability that bespoke his early discipline. Tennis and cricket also attracted him, indeed all the pastimes of his age and generation found him an eager adherent.

The King passed out of Dartmouth in December 1912 when he was just seventeen years old. In those days it was the practice of the Admiralty to send cadets who had completed their shore courses to sea in order to gain their sea experience before becoming midshipmen—this is contradistinction to the present custom of drafting cadets into the various units of the navy and letting them work up to their promotion date with already gazetted midshipmen in the gun-room. The cadet ship of that year was *Cumberland*, as she had been for several years previously. *Cumberland* was a county cruiser of 9000 tons then under the command of Captain Aubrey Smith, now Admiral Sir Aubrey Clare Smith. Captain (then Commander) H. Spencer-Cooper, who had been one of the King's Instructors at Dartmouth, and later was to write the account of the Falkland Island Battle, was appointed to the ship also, to be in especial attendance on the King, and on board there were some sixty other cadets completing their preliminary training in the same way as the King. The mere fact that the King was sent on this voyage emphasized the intention that he should serve his way regularly up the Navy as his father had done before him. Quite a different plan, on the contrary, had been adopted with regard to the Duke of Windsor, who as soon as he passed out of Dartmouth had been posted as a midshipman to *Hindustan*, thus indicating that it was not proposed that he should continue a naval career very much longer.

The voyage of *Cumberland*, which began on January 18th, 1913, covered a very wide cruising area. The ship touched at Teneriffe, St. Lucia, Trinidad, Barbados, Martinique (only a few years after the eruption that blasted St. Pierre to oblivion), Dominica, Puerta Rica, Jamaica (which the King was to visit under very different circumstances fourteen years later), Havana, Bermuda, in the West Indies, as well as several of the Canadian and Newfoundland ports. Through the cruise there was plenty of opportunity for enjoyment as well as for the assimilation of knowledge, and the King did not miss any of his chances. The fact that the King's son was on board *Cumberland* gave an added incentive to the people of the various cities to entertain the personnel, and great must have been the festivity, especially in Canada, which Dominion he was the first of the King George's sons to visit. There is one episode that occurred in Montreal which throws a cheerful light on the King's love of fun. The occasion was an official one, so Commander Spencer-Cooper, as he then was, naturally anxious that the dignitaries of the city—both French and British—should feel that they were being treated on an absolute equality, busied himself with finding partners for the King from the ranks of their daughters. Being a Naval cadet first and a King's son afterwards, the King had other views as to the proper way to enjoy a dance, and his partners, though excelling in charm, were not exclusively drawn from the official ranks. The Commander was in despair that his well-intentioned efforts should come to naught, when an accident, lucky for everybody but himself, set things merrily on the right path. He was of course in full Naval uniform, frock-coat, encircling belt, and all. In his perturbation and exertion, both brace-buttons at the back parted company with his trousers. There was no way of repairing the damage *coram populo*, and the only way in which he could preserve the decencies was by an occasional convulsive hitch to his waist-belt through the enveloping folds of his frock-coat. Fearful that his charge might think he had suddenly given way to a peculiar mania, the Commander hastened to tell the King of his dilemma. That was enough. There were no more languishing partners. The King impishly saw to it that everybody with whom he could possibly dance was told of the contretemps and the rest of that ball was what in colloquial language is known as a " howling success "—even if the howls were howls of laughter.

On the completion of the *Cumberland* cruise the King was gazetted midshipman and appointed to *Collingwood*, then the flagship of the first battle squadron (Vice-Admiral, now Admiral, Sir Stanley Colville) with Captain (now Admiral) James Ley in command. He joined her at Rosyth in September and next month was in the Mediterranean for a two months' cruise—memorable to the King in that while the squadron was in Egyptian waters he stayed with Lord Kitchener. Malta, too, held memories when he revisited there on the way home in *Renown* in 1927.

The fateful year of 1914 opened quite normally with Fleet exercises at Portsmouth, and the spring and summer training was carried out at Lamlash in the Isle of Arran. Still following the ordinary routine the Fleet was back in Devonport in June to prepare for the great review in July which preceded by only a few weeks the outbreak of the Great War.

The King brought to *Collingwood* the same enviable reputation he had enjoyed at Dartmouth and on *Cumberland*. Always anxious that he should be treated as one of the ship's company, always ready for his full share of whatever was going in the way of work, he took his place in the gun-room in the same way as any other of the score or so of midshipmen who served. The routine was the same for him as for all the rest. Turn out at six o'clock with just time for a hasty basin of cocoa before physical drill; bath and breakfast; divisions; working parties with the ratings or in the schoolroom with the Instructor—all the many duties that fall to the lot of the midshipmen through the day and at the end slinging his own hammock. On such occasions as coaling ship—for the oil burner was then somewhat of a rarity in the Navy—the King became like all the rest a " red-eyed black demon with flashing teeth " labouring in the pitch-black hold of a dingy collier, where the bags were sent down in slings to be filled, and shot skyward again before the next lot came down. The King was there to take a hand with the rest, for coaling is a very serious business where " records " are to be established and kept and where, if the work lags, the afterguard take their turn with the ratings. Captain W. E. C. Tait, now commanding H.M.S. *Shropshire*, who was in the *Collingwood* with him, draws a vivid sketch of him on such occasions. " He always put his back into whatever was going," he says, " and I can see him now, rushing through the intense effort of the day and then finishing up with the traditional bread and cheese, onions, and beer before turning in. All his work was done cheerfully and well, but perhaps best of all was the way he handled the picket boat when he was in charge of her, while he was more than a good hand at the sailing races."

His brother midshipmen give him just the same character. "He was never one to push himself forward," one of them has summed him up, "but he would fight to the last ditch for a pal." The gun-room and ward-room alike respected his earnestly expressed wish that nothing should be said or done that would in the slightest degree set him in a place apart. They carried out that wish even to the extent of inventing a name for him. Ordinarily and on the more formal occasions he was, of course, Prince Albert, but among themselves he was known as "Mr. Johnston," and he answered to that in gun-room and ward-room. Indeed even the ratings used the sobriquet on occasion, and as one of his fellow officers said: "I have heard a messenger come to the gun-room door to say that the Commander wanted Mr. Johnston and seen the King get up and go out without comment."

But the incident which perhaps more than anything else emphasized this attitude occurred shortly after the outbreak of war, when King George V came to visit his fleet and boarded *Collingwood*. When the inspection was over His Majesty, according to custom, received the officers of the ship on the quarter-deck. The Captain introduced them in strict order of seniority, and among the ranks of the juniors was Prince Albert, in line after the Sub-Lieutenants and with his colleagues of the gun-room. Father and son had not met for some time, but no watcher would even know that relation existed between them. Midshipman Prince Albert passed his King with the click of heels and salute that every one in the line had given. No word was spoken.

CHAPTER THREE

WAR SERVICE

A MONTH after war broke out, the illness which was for so many years to be so severe a handicap to the King manifested itself seriously, and he had to be put on board the hospital ship *Rohilla* and from her landed at Aberdeen. He was hurried into a nursing home and operated on for appendicitis, though it was subsequently discovered that this disease was only a subsidiary cause of the attacks of violent pain from which he suffered. He had fought against giving in so long, however, that the operation and its effect on a constitution weakened by resistance kept him an invalid for several weeks. Fretting to get back to active service afloat he worried the Naval Medical Board to pass him as fit in December, but they were adamant, and the best he could do was to be sent for service at the Admiralty in the Operations Division. He was there for only five weeks, however, before the Medical Board relented, and in February 1915 he rejoined his ship at Portsmouth and went in her to the main rendezvous of the Fleet at Scapa. He was even then by no means a well man, and from the first week of his rejoining the ship the attacks that had compelled his leaving her at the beginning of hostilities again manifested themselves. It was a heart-breaking time for him altogether and it needed more than ordinary determination to see the thing through. It was nine months before he had to acknowledge himself beaten and consent to be put ashore again, after the weary months of waiting in the Northern mists for the enemy to appear, nine months of rumours and ever-recurrent disappointments, amid the hard conditions imposed on naval life afloat at that period of the war. But even ashore the King would not neglect his duties and " go sick " any more than he was absolutely compelled to do. He spent the winter on shore certainly, but not always as an invalid. Most alarming statements were occasionally published by the newspapers as to the real state of his health, but whenever and wherever he could, he relieved his father of some of his official functions in that anxious and desperate time, and just as soon as ever he could " get back to his job " he went back to the Admiralty to serve in the Operations Division for three months in the early part of 1916. Then, in May of that year, to his unbounded delight he was allowed to rejoin his ship, just a few weeks before the battle of Jutland.

Though not so heavily engaged as some others of the High Sea Fleet, *Collingwood* had quite a brisk time in that battle. She was in the 5th Division of the First Battle Squadron, and on the day of the action was second ship to the flagship *Colossus*, *Neptune* and *St. Vincent* being the others in the line. When contact was first made with the enemy, on the afternoon of May 31st, visibility was only about four miles with thick weather all about, and though firing could be heard and occasional flashes seen on the skyline nothing definite could be distinguished until shortly after six o'clock, when the gun flashes became more frequent and a few minutes later an enemy cruiser came in sight. She had evidently already been engaged and was apparently stopped. There was only time for a few rounds, however, at about 9000 yards, when the mist closed down and she was lost sight of behind the veil. In that time, however, there were some observers on board *Collingwood* who thought that the firing had got home and that the cruiser was sunk—that will never be known now. It was then growing so thick that neither guns nor directors could be laid with certainty on the target. Momentarily the German line of battle could be seen, but there was a British Squadron between them and *Collingwood*. That squadron comprised the ill-fated *Defence* and *Black Prince*. The laconic official despatch of Admiral Ley to the Commander-in-Chief, tells a tale, reading between the lines, of the real tragedy of modern naval warfare. In two sentences there is the story: "They were firing vigorously, themselves on fire and repeatedly hit. The *Defence* was seen to blow up about 6.40." That is quite a classic in its brevity and in the complete picture it presents of the final catastrophe that overwhelmed the plucky ship.

Before many more minutes were passed a number of German destroyers made a torpedo attack on the

THE KING WITH THE DUKE OF WINDSOR AT A
FARMERS' MEET

Vandyck

AS GROUP CAPTAIN OF THE R.A.F.

fifth squadron from the rear and *Collingwood* brought her four-inchers into action against one of them which ventured too closely. This destroyer attack was possibly intended by the Germans to divert the attention of the 5th Division from some heavily damaged battle-cruisers which almost immediately came into sight, just after *Colossus* had been struck forward by a heavy shell. One or two salvoes fell between her and *Collingwood* and a spent heavy projectile ricocheted and burst between the two ships. *Collingwood* was not hit and the shell which burst above *Colossus* did little damage. These shells and the torpedo attack were the forerunner for the appearance out of the mist of two or three German warships. One of the cruisers was identified by observers on both *Collingwood* and *Colossus* as the *Derfflinger* or of that class. She presented a clear target at a range of about 8000 yards and fire was immediately opened on her by both the English ships, which shifted their attention from the destroyer to the bigger game. The *Derfflinger* was hit immediately by several shells which started fires and silenced all the guns except the fore-turret. *Collingwood* was using lyddite shell at the time and unfortunately before the charges could be shifted to A.P. shell, the *Derfflinger* disappeared into a dense smoke screen thrown out by several destroyers which surrounded the lame duck and escorted her out of range. She was seen to be listing heavily as she disappeared and it is significant that Admiral Sheer, in his first report to the Kaiser after the battle specially excepts the *Derfflinger* and the *Seydlitz* when he undertakes to have the German High Sea Fleet ready to take the sea again in two months' time, so that *Collingwood's* adversary must have been very badly damaged, because we know that only good seamanship got the *Seydlitz* back to Kiel, and therefore the *Derfflinger* must have been in just as parlous a state. This was the last of the action as far as *Collingwood* was concerned except that a little while later a few rounds from the main armament were put into a damaged enemy destroyer. Altogether, *Collingwood* expended eighty-four rounds and did her bit towards the triumph of the British Navy.

For his coolness and courage under fire the King was mentioned in despatches. He was serving in " A " 12-inch turret—the fore-turret—and it needs nerve to go through hour after hour of action stations in a battleship's turret, far more nerve than is required from officers serving in gunnery control positions or on the bridge. The turret crew know nothing of what is going on. In the close confines of their steel pen the only words that come down to them are the quiet directions of the gunnery officer, droned through a telephone giving range and elevation for the fixing of the guns on a target the gun crew never see, whose character they never know. The petty officer at the receiver end of the telephone repeats the orders, the gun-layer twists a few controls and the heavy breeches swing obediently into position. There is a crisp click as the trigger is released and the huge bulk of the 12-incher recoils on its bearings as the charge sends the huge shell hurtling through the air. The acrid smell of the lyddite fills the chamber, a few wisps of it drift back from the muzzle or from the breech as it is swung open, and sponging gear cleanses the rifling. Clanging up from the magazines comes the next charge on its chain conveyor, first the shell and then the bags of lyddite. Rapidly they are pushed into the breech, ponderously that breech swings to with a sound as of safe doors locking. There is a momentary hush and then the breech begins once again its blind seeking for its prey. The crew can only guess what is going on. A clamorous thud on the outside of the turret may tell them they are under fire and hit. A lurch and quiver of the ship may hint that a shell or a torpedo has found its way to a vital part. Any moment may see their walls of feet-thick steel bulge and burst and the crew in a red heap of horror on the deck. The enemy may be below the skyline or close alongside, may be attacking strongly or fleeing the onslaught. The gun crew cannot know. They serve the gun and wait. In such surroundings the King spent hour after hour on that fateful day and far into the night. Asked whether there was anything special he could remember about the day, the officer in charge of the turret could not recall anything outside the ordinary routine of duties gone through as though the ship was on firing practice in some peaceful stretch of the Atlantic. " Oh yes," he said as an afterthought, " I remember the King made cocoa as usual for me and the gun crew." He made cocoa !

It was just part of his job and he did it. And to-day one of his treasured possessions is the white ensign *Collingwood* flew at the battle.

Not long afterwards, the old gastric trouble again supervened and he spent many weary weeks on hospital ships in Scapa Flow. But not idly. He saw no reason why if a hard Fate condemned him to his back he should not continue his studies, and every day from the schoolroom of *Collingwood* came papers in seamanship and other subjects set for his special benefit, or else a schedule of work to be done in order that he might keep abreast of his colleagues. And always there was in existence a complete organization for taking him back from the hospital ship to *Collingwood* in case the Germans should venture forth again. He meant not to miss any chance of active service that should come his way, and one can prophesy had the Germans come out that the King would have been at his station on his ship within the hour. With the approach of winter, however, the illness grew worse and the doctors had to insist on his remaining ashore, unwilling as they well might be to sanction his remaining in the cold hard rigours of the Northern winters in ships on active service. As soon as he was anyway fit again he joined the staff of the Commander-in-Chief at Portsmouth and threw himself into his new work with characteristic energy. It attracted him enormously, and he says of it himself that the duties he then carried out and the way in which he was employed by Sir Stanley Colville made this period the most interesting time he had all through the war.

The winter over, he went back to sea again, this time as an acting-Lieutenant in the battleship *Malaya*. She was with the Fifth Battle Squadron at Scapa Flow and the King found that once more his duties took him into one of the big gun turrets. There was no sign of the enemy being inclined again to test their full strength against the British fleet, which lay, so far as its first line units were concerned, inactive through the summer in Scapa Flow. The disheartening gastric trouble kept visiting the King, and in November 1917 duodenal ulcer was definitely diagnosed and immediate operation advised. The three doctors who signed nearly all King George V's bulletins during his first illness, Lord Dawson of Penn, Colonel Sir Hugh Rigby, and Sir Stanley Hewett—together with the late Sir Frederick Treves—were the consultants, and Sir Hugh Rigby performed the operation which was in the event definitely to terminate his sea career. At first it was thought that with returning strength and the removal of the root of all the trouble, he might look forward to going to sea again after a year ashore. That was in itself a keen disappointment, but later it was to be realized that the severe nature of the operation and the after effect of it on a constitution weakened as it had been previously by the long unavailing fight against giving in to the advance of the disease, would preclude his ever making the Navy his permanent profession.

Just as soon as he was convalescent, he began to harry the authorities for something to do. The feverish development of the air services—both the Royal Flying Corps and the Royal Naval Air Service —offered an opportunity. The R.N.A.S. was only too anxious to secure the services of young, well-trained naval officers to look after the ground personnel while pilots were being turned out by the hundred to satisfy the enormous demands made for them by the forces. The King gladly seized the chance of carrying on in some way the old familiar conditions of his war service and working again among men of his own kidney. In February 1918 he was appointed to the R.N.A.S. station at Cranwell, where he remained until July. The higher commands were at that time decidedly at odds as to the control of Great Britain's war effort in the air, and it will be remembered how keen was the controversy and how loath the Admiralty was to let the administration of their own very effective arm pass from their hands. But the exigencies of the intense effort of the last year of the war overcame their objections in the end and the Royal Naval Air Service was in April amalgamated with the Royal Flying Corps to become the Royal Air Force. The R.N.A.S. station at Cranwell was one of the first places to come under the new regime and the King as he was serving there was one of the first batch of Naval Officers to be absorbed into the R.A.F., his rank being Captain, R.A.F.

There were only a few more months remaining

for active service. In August the King went with the R.A.F. Cadet Brigade to Hastings and later to Shorncliffe, crossing to France in October on his appointment to the Independent Air Force which then had its headquarters at Nancy. He served there till the Armistice on the Staff of General Sir Hugh Trenchard, now Marshal of the Royal Air Force, Viscount Trenchard.

His first official, or rather Royal, duty after the Armistice was to represent His Majesty King George V at the spectacular entry into Brussels of the King of the Belgians in November 1918. Later he was transferred to the Staff of Sir Hugh Salmond and spent Christmas at Spa in Belgium, remaining there under ordinary service conditions until he returned to England in February 1919. From field work to office work was a natural transition in those hard-working days after the Armistice when the work of four years in the massing of men to fight had to be undone and destroyed in as many months. He spent a month or so at the Air Ministry going through several sub-departments in his desire to accumulate experience. He told the Civil Service Association in a later year that he made so many changes in that short time that he felt like a buff slip —" Passed to you for action please." But in the process of being moved about from one room to another he managed to amass a great deal of intimate knowledge of how a Government Department was or should be conducted.

Then when he had absorbed all that he could of

ground and office conditions in the R.A.F. he began his training for a Pilot's certificate, passing his flying tests in July. Altogether he had a very busy time in that summer, for in addition to his R.A.F. service and training he was called on for many official duties to help King George V and the Duke of Windsor. He was appointed a Squadron Leader of the R.A.F. in August 1919, and in the same month he retired from the active list of both the Royal Navy and the R.A.F. There had been some discussion as to whether he might not go back to sea as was his own wish, but it was felt that with so many thousands of young officers being demobilized and turned again into civil life the situation might be regarded as somewhat incongruous, and it was finally decided that instead he should, like so many of them, be given a course at Cambridge.

It was not, however, until 1921 that the final indication of his retirement from a naval life occurred, when he was gazetted as Commander in January. He had not then done the three years sea service which is necessary before a regular Naval officer can be sure of his step. His father, King George V, had, on the other hand, served more than the full term at sea (four years to be exact) before he was promoted. In the ordinary way the King has " gone up " the three services since then. He was Captain in the Navy in 1925, Rear-Admiral in 1932, and Admiral in 1936. In the Royal Air Force he was appointed Wing Commander in 1920, Group Captain in 1921, Air Vice-Marshal in 1932,

WAR SERVICE

Air Marshal on January 1st, 1936, and Air Chief Marshal in June 1936. In the Army his appointments have all been honorary. He was gazetted Major-General in 1932 and General in 1936. On his accession in December 1936 he assumed the ranks of Admiral of the Fleet, Colonel-in-Chief of the Royal Marines, Field-Marshal and Marshal of the Royal Air Force, Colonel-in-Chief of the Life Guards, Royal Horse Guards, Royal Regiment of Artillery, the Corps of Royal Engineers, the Grenadier Guards, the Coldstream Guards, the Scots Guards, the Irish Guards, the Welsh Guards, and Captain-General of the Royal Territorial Army. He is also Colonel-in-Chief of the 11th Hussars, the Somerset Light Infantry, the East Yorks Regiment, and the Royal Army Ordnance Corps, and Honorary Colonel of the 4th Battalion Queen's Own Cameron Highlanders and the Leicestershire Yeomanry.

CHAPTER FOUR

UNIVERSITY LIFE AND HIS HONOURS

IN the year after the Armistice the daily papers announced that " some hundreds of the younger naval officers whose education had been interrupted by the war are now to be sent to various colleges at Cambridge to continue their studies." That decision inspired one of Rudyard Kipling's best post-war poems. He called it " The Scholars," and many of its lines live in the memory.

They have taken the men who were careless lads in Dartmouth
    in fourteen
And entered them into the landward schools as though no war
    had been ;
They have piped the children off all the seas from the Falklands
    to the Bight
And quartered them on the colleges to learn to read and write.

Their books were rain and sleet and fog—the dry gale and the
    snow,
Their teachers were the horned mine and the humped-back
    death below ;
Their schools were walled by the walking mists and roofed by
    the waiting skies
When they conned their task in a new-sown field with the Moon-
    light Sacrifice.

They have touched a knowledge outreaching speech—as when
    the cutters were sent
To harvest the dreadful mile of beach after the Vanguard went.

They have learnt great faith and little fear and a high heart in
    distress,
And how to suffer each sodden year of heaped-up weariness.
They have borne the bridle upon their lips and the yoke upon
    their neck
Since they went down to the sea in ships to save a world from
    wreck.

Far have they come, much have they braved. Give them their
    hour of play
While the hidden things their hands have saved work for them
    night and day.

.   .   .   .

Till the grateful past their youth redeemed return them their
    youth once more.

The King, no less than his colleagues and fellow-
undergraduates, had seen the grimness of it all. He,
no less than they, had rubbed shoulders with Death ;
had seen the deep horror of it all ; had listened to
half-told tales in gun-room and ward-room from
boys of his own age who had gone down with a
smile on their lips and a jest in their hearts to
unimagined hells. It was then fitting that he as well
as they should round off his war service with the
gentle, quiet, and hallowed surroundings of University tradition. So he and his brother, Prince Henry
Duke of Gloucester, went up to Cambridge in 1919,
" to complete their education," and to live the ordinary care-free, cheery life of the undergraduate,
unhampered by any of the divinity that once did
hedge a King—to paraphrase a quotation that the
British Royal Family have done more to discount
than any other in the whole world.

The King leased a house in Cambridge, where he and his brother lived in preference to going into residence at Trinity College. With them lived Wing Commander Sir Louis Greig and Mrs. Greig, to supervise their domestic and general comfort. Wing Commander Greig had been associated with the King for many years by that time, and was to end his official connection with him as the Controller of his Household. The association began at Osborne, where Wing Commander Greig was then serving as a medical officer, and was more than once called in to attend the King in his troublesome gastric attacks. They were together again in *Cumberland* during the cadet cruise and their naval careers again crossed when the King was appointed to *Malaya* and found Sir Louis Greig serving on board her. Indeed it was on the latter's strong advice that the King finally consented to the operation for duodenal ulcer. Wing Commander Greig, however, had actually no liking for a surgeon's life, and a month or two after the King had joined the Air Force in 1918 he transferred to that arm also, as Major. Thenceforward their ways again lay together for quite a number of years, and the friendship then founded has lasted as firmly as ever till to-day.

It cannot be said that either the King or his brother continued their studies uninterrupted by any extraneous influences. They were at Cambridge not to go through the three or four years necessary for a degree, but to take special courses in subjects that would fit them better for the exacting duties that they, as the King's sons, would be called on to perform in later years. The King himself took the special subjects that even so early in his life had begun to interest him deeply—history, economics, and civics—and those lectures consolidated and vitalized that interest, with the result we see to-day in his firm grasp of the essentials of industrial and manufacturing problems with their attendant requirements regarding the welfare of the workers and the care of their dependants. He went to those lectures as an ordinary student—on a bicycle, which then, as now, was the favourite form of locomotion in the University city. There was no pomp and circumstance—there never has been—about his coming and going, and his gown was as dusty and his cap as awry as those of any of his colleagues. Nor did he neglect the usual ambitions of the undergraduate in the matter of attracting the attention of the proctors. As he announced proudly in a speech after he had left the College, he had been fined for the heinous offence of smoking in the street while wearing his cap and gown—or as he himself put it, " The proctor's bull-dog once took six and eightpence out of me."

His life, though, at Cambridge was not all a placid progress from day to day of lectures, reading, and amusement. The Duke of Windsor was for part of the time away in Canada and, later, on his Australian tour, and many of the functions which he would have ordinarily performed fell to the lot of the King, who, in consequence, made many trips to London and was away from Cambridge a good deal during his time there. But he contrived to put in a very large amount of solid study and reading, and when he finally went down, he found himself thoroughly grounded in his favourite themes and their cognate subjects such as State and Property, Capital and Labour, Housing, Welfare of the Workers, Good Citizenship, and others. He had too the beginnings of a very extensive library dealing with all such matters, and to that library he has consistently added in order that he may keep himself abreast of every recent development or changed outlook.

His University course finished, the time had come for the King to take his full share of the many public duties which so far his father and his elder brother had borne almost unaided. He himself had been preoccupied with his war service and his University studies, or handicapped by his illness, though as has been said there were many occasions when he deputized for either the King or the Heir Apparent. But from now onwards he was to come before the public much more frequently and under far more important conditions than he had done heretofore. Soon after he left the University, he was " raised to the Peerage," a statement which seems hard to reconcile with the fact that he was a Prince of the Blood Royal. But that distinction does not entitle him to a seat and a vote in the

House of Lords, any more than does the honour of being a Knight of the Garter. To that first Order of Chivalry, he had been elected by the King on his twenty-first birthday. It was the only British title he then held, for unlike the Dukedom of Cornwall, which is an hereditary title of the Prince of Wales, the Dukedom of York, though always bestowed on a King's son or brother, has to be conferred. This was done in the birthday honours list of June 1920, and on the 23rd of that month he took his seat in the House of Lords, twenty-eight years almost to the day since his father had done so.

The title Duke of York goes far back in English history, its creation dating from 1385 when King Richard II conferred it on his brother Edmund Langley, for his campaign against the Scots. There had been Earls of Yorkshire in the peerage before, but the House of York was founded by Edmund Langley, and his blood has been in the veins of every holder of the title since then up to the present time. For nearly a hundred years it was an hereditary title, the last to hold it thus being Edward of Rouen, who inherited it from his father Richard Plantagenet when the latter fell on the field of Wakefield. When his son became King Edward IV the title merged into a Royal honour, and from that day onwards has remained in the gift of the Sovereigns to confer upon a son or brother. From that limitation it follows that the title has several times lapsed. It was, for example, in abeyance for the whole of the sixteenth century until 1605, when it was revived by James I for Charles Stuart, who held it as a sickly lad for seven years until the death of his elder brother Henry made him Prince of Wales. Since then it has lapsed six times for periods ranging from sixty-five years (1827 to 1892 when King George V was made Duke of York) to nineteen years, the time which elapsed between the date when His Majesty relinquished the title to the date when it was bestowed upon his son. In strict chronology, and having regard only to recognized holders of the title, there is a shorter period than nineteen years when there was no Duke of York to sit in the House of Lords. That was from 1767 to 1784 between the two Hanoverians, Edward Augustus and Frederic Augustus, brother and son respectively of George III. But during those years there was a Duke of York alive, who though England did not credit him was, nevertheless, honoured as such by the Papacy, by Louis XV and by other continental nations. That holder—sometimes called the Bogus Duke—was the second son of the old Pretender, " James the Third of England " —" the King Here " as the Romans called him to distinguish him from King George the First, " the King There." That son was baptized by Pope Benedict XIV himself in the names of Henry Benedict Maria Clement Stewart, " I present to your Holiness the Duke of York," said the old Pretender, " that you may make him a Christian." The " Duke " was to enter the Church of Rome a

TO LECTURES ON A MOTOR BICYCLE

THE KING AND QUEEN AT THE TIME OF THEIR ENGAGEMENT

year or so after the hopes of his elder brother, Bonnie Prince Charlie, had been shattered at Culloden, to become a Cardinal two days after he had received the tonsure, and a week later to become a Prince of the Church. That was the death-blow to the hopes of the Jacobites who nevertheless recognized him when Prince Charles died—as King Henry IX of England.

Curiously enough the old Pretender touches other facets of the Dukedom of York. The holder of the title of the Dukedom of York has for subsidiary titles Earl of Inverness and Baron Killarney. There does not seem much of consequence centring round the latter title, but there is a tang of romance about the Earldom of Inverness. For that dignity the old Pretender had a fondness, for he conferred it certainly upon one and probably upon two of his devoted adherents. The first to have it was John Hay of Cromlix, who fled the country after the Jacobite rising of 1715, joined the Court of " James III " and was made Earl of Inverness by him in 1718. He died without heirs in 1740, and in 1759 James III is said to have conferred the title once more, this time upon the Hon. Alex Murray, the fourth son of Lord Elibank. " He," laconically says the chronicle, " took an active part against the Government in the Westminster election of 1750." In those days the Government did not like people who did so foolish a thing, and the audacious opposition speaker and worker had to flee to France, where he lived until 1777 under the title of Count

Murray. James created him an Earl, and the title was in all probability Earl of Inverness. The same title was to be used again in connection with a King's son, for it was conferred upon one of the sons of George III—Prince Frederic Augustus, as a supplement to his title of Duke of Sussex. Here again romance creeps in, for the Duke of Sussex married—as his second morganatic wife—Letitia Underwood, the daughter of an Earl of Arran, and she was made Duchess of Inverness by Queen Victoria in 1840, thus settling a perennial problem as to precedence. At functions thereafter she ranked "immediately before the senior Marchioness."

There is coincidence also in the King's election to his second order of Knighthood—the Thistle—on the occasion of his marriage to a Scotch bride. This order was revived by a King of England— James II—who was himself a Duke of York, after, according to tradition, it had remained in abeyance from the early days when King Achaius of Scotland founded it to commemorate a victory over Athelstan, King of the Saxons. The warrant relating to the Order mentions this fact, though hard-headed antiquaries discount the tradition. Still the Thistle is the second Order of Knighthood in Great Britain, older by nearly a century than the Order of St. Patrick and junior only to the Garter, the most ancient and most illustrious Order of Chivalry in the whole of Europe. It was founded by Edward III, the sovereign whose son created the first Duke of York, though it was a Lancastrian, Henry IV,

who is hailed as " the great restorer of the honour
of the Order." The King completed the trilogy of
the three orders of chivalry when he became Knight
of St. Patrick in 1936. In addition to the three
British Orders of Chivalry, the King is a Knight of
Justice of the Order of the Hospital of St. John of
Jerusalem in England, and his foreign orders include
the Grand Cross of the Order of Carol I of Roumania,
and the Order of St. Vladimir of Russia. He is
a Knight Grand Cross of the Royal Victorian Order,
founded by Queen Victoria for personal service to
the Sovereign or members of the Royal Family,
and a Knight Grand Cross of the Order of St.
Michael and St. George, the order recognized
as rewarding Imperial services until the Order of
the British Empire was founded, to take some of
the ever-widening circle of such servants of the
Empire. The Duke was awarded the order just
previous to his world trip of 1927, when he visited
Australia. Finally he became a member of the
Privy Council in 1925, and a member of the Council
of State erected during the severe illness of King
George V in 1929, and again in 1936.

From the very first holder of the title, romance
and tragedy, history, and high emprise have centred
round the Dukes of York all through the pages of
English history to a like, perhaps even to a greater
degree than the drama which surrounds the Princes
of Wales. Six of them in their day and generation
succeeded to the English throne—Edward IV,
Henry VIII, Charles I, James II, George V, and

now George VI. Two have died in battle, the second Duke, Edward, the son of that Edmund Langley, first holder of the title, who fell fighting bravely, though an old man, at Agincourt in 1415, and Richard Plantagenet, slain at Wakefield after being the virtual ruler of England during the mental malady of Henry VI, and the father of two future Kings of England—Edward IV and Richard III. One has been murdered, one executed, two exiled, and another two, Edward IV " the Don Juan King," and Henry VIII have gone down to posterity as among the greatest lovers in the world.

CHAPTER FIVE

MARRIAGE

IN his book *The Dukes of York*, Mr. Graham Brooks says: " One thing the present Duke has in common with his predecessors. Whilst the Princes of Wales have almost invariably been compelled to accept the brides that State policy selected, the Dukes of York have nearly always obeyed the dictates of their hearts. The first Duke met his future wife upon a lonely strip of road in Southern France, the romance of the latest Duke is still with us."

That romance began in the closing years of the war, when the King was still Prince Albert, and the Queen was Lady Elizabeth Bowes-Lyon, the youngest daughter of the Earl and Countess of Strathmore, one of the oldest families of the Scottish aristocracy. The line goes back to the dimness of unwritten history, for Scottish knights in the days of chivalry had not chroniclers so precise as their brothers across the Border. But the Strathmore crest, in heraldic language, is " A lady to the girdle, richly habited, holding in her hand the Rose and Thistle." This crest commemorates the marriage of the Lady Jean Stewart, daughter of Robert II of Scotland, with Sir John Lyon of Forteviot, who in

1372 received from his King the Thanage of Glamis. To-day Glamis Castle is still in the cherished possession of the family. Tradition has it that it is in truth Macbeth's Castle, although no certain claim to that seat of high tragedy can be established. But there is an historical fact, apart altogether from legend, which gives the marriage of the King to Lady Elizabeth Bowes-Lyon a romantic coincidence as great as in any other story, for the first Duke of York won his title as a reward for his part in the English raid into Scotland in 1385 against the same Scottish King, Robert II, who gave his daughter Lady Jean to Sir John Lyon in 1372 and, as related above, made him Thane of Glamis. And so after five centuries and more the descendants of the founders of those two houses come together again in a union than which few have been more blessed with the true sentiment of British married life.

The future Queen of England had no hint in her earlier years that she was one day to be the first lady in the land. The youngest but one of a high-spirited family of ten, petted and bullied as all small girls must be by several sport and play-loving brothers, her life until the grim days of the war was compact of all the healthy happiness that is the peculiar heritage of the sons and daughters of English and Scottish landed families. She spent most of her childhood days at the family seat, St. Paul's Walden-bury in Hertfordshire, where she was born, though for three months in every year she was at Glamis

Castle, in those months when Scotland claims the holiday-seeking people, and there were, of course, the usual visits to country houses, to London and even abroad to Italy, where her grandmother lived. Except for two terms at a day-school she was educated almost entirely at home, first by her mother and then by a succession of governesses, until she passed the Junior Oxford Local. That was when she was fourteen, and in the same year war broke out and the tranquil, well-ordered life was rudely interrupted. Lessons still went on but there were other distractions : deep sorrow and strong feeling. Four of her brothers went away at once, one to find his death at Loos, another to languish in a German prison camp. Her sisters and her mother threw themselves into the many strenuous occupations in which the women of Britain so worthily strove. Glamis Castle itself was turned into a hospital. There the Lady Elizabeth would come to entertain the wounded, and to-day all over the world where " poor fighting men are nursing their scars," some account themselves luckier than their fellows because they happened to be sent to Glamis for their recovery. Right through the world tour, undertaken by the King and Queen in 1927, there were incidents—in New Zealand, in Australia and in Malta, where the Duchess met again those who had fought in France and, wounded or ill, had gone that long night journey to the North and found within the age-old walls of Glamis peace and loving-kindness. It was a time of stress and strain for a high-spirited, sympathetic girl striving all the time to keep up the spirits of war-weary men—but it was fine training in character and poise for one who was to be the wife of a King.

Though the hospital at Glamis remained opened until after the Armistice, the end of the war saw the Lady Elizabeth moving about a good deal more in society, and through the gay season of 1919, when on the surface people were trying to put the lean years of 1914–18 behind them, she was increasingly seen at balls and society functions in London. It was then that the King first met her as a " grown up " —they had known each other as children—and their friendship soon ripened into a deeper feeling. People began to notice how much they were seen together, and general public interest was stimulated when in August of next year the King paid his first visit to Glamis Castle, where there was a large house party to meet him. Sentimental curiosity was further whetted next year when Lady Elizabeth Bowes-Lyon was one of the bridesmaids of Princess Mary, and the speculations of the quidnuncs became almost a certainty when Queen Mary, with her son, visited Glamis Castle. Several months more elapsed, however, before the formal announcement of the engagement was made on January 16th, 1923, as a result of a proposal on the previous Sunday ; most appropriately in the grounds of St. Paul's Walden-bury, with its thronging memories of many hours of happiness. The Court Circular paragraph recorded the greatest pleasure of King George V and Queen Mary in announcing the betrothal of their beloved son to Lady Elizabeth Bowes-Lyon—" to which the King had gladly given his consent." The formalities were completed at a special meeting of the Privy Council on February 12th, when in pursuance of the Royal Marriage Act of 1772 a document was signed signifying the Royal consent " to the contracting of matrimony between His Royal Highness Albert Frederick Arthur George, Duke of York, and the Lady Elizabeth Angela Margaret Bowes-Lyon, youngest daughter of the Rt. Honourable Claude George, Earl of Strathmore and Kinghorne."

This formality was rendered necessary under the provisions of the Royal Marriage Act, which enacted that no descendant of King George II shall be capable of contracting matrimony without the previous consent of His Majesty, His Heirs or Successors, signified under the Great Seal. This Royal Marriage Act is one of the few remaining traces of the personal rule of the Hanoverian sovereigns, though it has been amended by recent legislation exempting the ex-King from its provisions. Most of those influences were swept away after or during the great war, when the House of Guelph became the House of Windsor and the German origin of the line was obliterated as far as possible. Among those legacies of the Georges was the ukase that Royal Princes must only marry royalties. King George announced that his younger children would be permitted to choose their consorts from the families of the first three ranks of the British nobility—Dukes, Marquesses, and Earls. Queen Victoria had allowed two of her daughters to do so and Princess Mary was the first of the House of Windsor to marry an English aristocrat. The King followed the same wise plan, to the very evident approval of the nation.

It is an interesting comment on the event that there had been an interval of two and a half centuries since last an English King had given his consent to a marriage of a Royal Prince in direct succession to the Throne, to one of his subjects. The Sovereign was Charles II, and the occasion was the marriage of his brother James II to Ann Hyde, the daughter of the Earl of Clarendon, in 1660. That union gave two queens to the English Throne, Queen Mary, the Consort of William III, and Queen Anne. Carrying the coincidence still further, James Duke of York was also a naval officer—Lord High Admiral of England—and a very efficient naval officer as well— as Samuel Pepys over and over again testifies. It is curious to turn up those references to-day, especially the record of his meeting with Mr. Coventry who "discoursed largely and bravely on the subject of the Duke,"—"that he is more himself and more of judgements is at hand in him in the middle of a desperate service, than at other times and though he is a man naturally martiall to the highest degree, yet a man that never in his life talks one word of service of his owne, but only that he saw such and such a thing and lays it down for maxime that a Hector can have no courage." Then there is Pepys' great rival as a diarist, John Evelyn. He can be quoted too—" I think him of a most sincere and honest nature." Words such as these could well be written of the King to-day.

The marriage of the King and Queen took place on a grey April day with fitful gleams of sunshine to shine upon a happy bride. It was solemnized in Westminster Abbey, by the Archbishop of Canterbury, the Archbishop of York delivering the address, while the Primate of Scotland was present at the ceremony among many other ecclesiastical dignitaries. The King was attended by his brothers, the then Prince of Wales and Prince Henry, and the bride, who was given away by her father, had six of her girlhood friends as bridesmaids—Lady Mary Cambridge, Lady May Cambridge, now Lady Abel-Smith, Lady Katharine Hamilton, Lady Mary Thynne, the Hon. Diamond Hardinge, and Miss Betty Cator, while her two nieces, the Hon. Elizabeth Elphinstone and the Hon. Cecilia Bowes-Lyon, were also in attendance. Most of that band of attendants have since followed in the footsteps of the bride herself. The public interest in the whole proceedings was intense. Huge crowds assembled from early morning, lining the whole route of the procession from the bride's house in Bruton Street and from Buckingham Palace all through Whitehall to the Abbey. Their enthusiasm was undimmed and everywhere vociferous, the popularity of the King and the charm of the Queen alike winning ungrudged tribute. All grades of British society from the highest orders of the aristocracy to the humble Cockney, who had walked cheerfully from the outer fringes of the East End, were united in the one desire—to show how very thoroughly they appreciated the fact that a King's son was marrying—and was marrying a fellow subject. Not the least delightful memory of that day was the sight of H.M. King George V himself and his unaffected pride and pleasure in the marriage of his second son. It was not a sovereign surveying the union of a Prince of the blood Royal—it was a father beaming with affection for a well-loved son. The honeymoon was spent first at Polesden Lacey, then at Glamis Castle, and finally at Frogmore, before the King and his bride came back to London and took up their residence at White Lodge, Richmond Park. The Queen was the second of the title to live there, for it had been there that Queen Mary was staying as the Duchess of York, when her eldest son was born. Still more was it associated with Queen Mary, for her own childhood was spent there, and it was also the residence of her mother, the Duchess of Teck.

The time had now come for the King to enter fully into the arduous task of a Royalty—meeting the many public calls upon his time and his energy, taking some of the burden from the shoulders of his father and his brother and developing for himself new avenues of interest and enthusiasm. That task was rendered all the more smooth because of the very genuine, very affectionate regard with which the public from the first surrounded the young couple, whose happiness in each other and in their life was so patently and so charmingly reflected in all they did. The one remaining event which completed that public approval and their private happiness alike was the birth to them in 1926 of the little Princess Elizabeth. Never has a baby girl attracted more love and notice. From the day she was born there were always groups waiting outside the door of that house in Bruton Street whence her mother went as a bride, hoping for a glimpse of " the fourth lady in the land." Her journeys in the park and thereabouts were triumphal progresses, her outgoings and incomings one of the treasured London sights.

As she grew and was joined by her sister Margaret Rose, who was born in 1930, to complete that ideal family circle which has ever since been honoured and beloved throughout the whole of the Empire, the interest in the two delightful daughters has never waned. Their babyhood, their small girl days and ways, have been watched and faithfully chronicled by scores of writers for the interest and edification of millions of readers. Wherever they happened to be staying—at 145 Piccadilly, at the Royal Lodge, Windsor, staying with her adoring Grandmother the Queen Mother (whom Princess Elizabeth so strikingly resembles) or at the various country houses they visit, there is sure to be found a knot of people about the entrance, hoping for the chance of a glimpse of the Royal children. Keen photographers scheme for an opportunity to " snap " them even to the length of invading the next door house and photographing them over the wall or through a window as they play happily in their own garden. Hardly a day passes without some item of news about them appearing in the public prints—their sayings, their doings, their visits, and above all the thousand and one marks of affection lavished on them by their parents and others. From the day of her birth the King and, especially, the Queen have realised the possibilities of the situation that has now become a reality, and have trained the Princess Elizabeth—and the Princess Margaret Rose has naturally shared in the training—in all the attributes and the accomplishments which would help her to bear the burden of monarchy should it ever fall on her shoulders. Her studies have their serious side, some intensive courses in languages, in the comportment of Royal Hostesses, and a wider knowledge of history than the ordinary ten-year-old school girl usually acquires. But though the two work hard they also play hard. There is no more happy hour spent by the King than in company of his two daughters, helping them to enjoy themselves with a whole-hearted appreciation of their ideas of fun, and, it is certain, more, much more than the mere conception of a father's duty to make his children happy. Whatever the game, he joins in and, perhaps, thinks out pranks and variations of his own which add to the joyfulness of the play hours. It is, one would think, a lasting grief with him that height makes it inconvenient for him to enter the doorway of the little model house which the people of Wales presented to the two Princesses. There they play for hours at being housewives, whenever they are at the Royal Lodge where the house is set up with two realistic Welsh dolls on the lawn in front, giving it the requisite air of "artistic verisimilitude." The Princess is perhaps more self-possessed than her younger sister, who is the more volatile of the two. From the day of Margaret Rose's birth the elder sister took it upon herself to "bring up the child in the way it should go," or at any rate to share in that task. Many are the stories, more numerous, perhaps, are the photographs of the two sisters in all manner of situations always unaffected, always sweet, always true to their birth and their breeding. Books have been written, books will be written about their sayings and doings, but here one memory must be recalled. On the occasion of the marriage of her uncle the Duke of Kent, the Princess Elizabeth was occupying the responsible position of a bridesmaid and very naturally was impressed with the importance of the appointment and the duties which it imposed on her. Her younger sister had no such restraining influence, nor was she noticeably impressed by the solemnity of Westminster Abbey. Seated on a cushion at her mother's feet, she was unaffectedly interested in all her surroundings— from the candles on the high altar to the arrival of all the notabilities, some of whom she knew and whose attention she vainly endeavoured to catch. An unruly skirt—short skirts worn by small girls *will* ride up above the knees—kept her engaged from time to time and the restraining touch of her mother reminded her that she was in church. When the Royal wedding party drew up the aisle to their appointed places Princess Margaret Rose quickly discovered her sister, cumbered about with the cares of a bridesmaid's onerous tasks. Desperately she tried to attract Princess Elizabeth's attention but the latter, mindful at once of the dignity of her position and the consequences that might follow from any unbending on her part, refused to even recognize Princess Margaret Rose's "well meant but misguided enthusiasm." Until at last, caught off guard, she did look in her younger sister's direction. Immediately a broad smile spread over the face of Princess Margaret Rose and, delightedly, she twiddled her fingers in a happy wave of greeting to her sister. She had accomplished her object and thereafter comparative quiet reigned in her Royal Highness's corner.

It is not alone in the English and Empire press and reading circles that the career of the two young princesses is faithfully chronicled. Their fame and their fascination have spread to the Continent and to the United States, and dwellers in other parts of the world outside the British Empire read, from time to time, and always with appreciation of the sayings and the doings of the two little ladies who play such an unaffected part in the enlivenment of the interest and the popularity which so happily surrounds the whole of the ideal family, who have endeared themselves so worthily to the Empire in particular and generally to the whole world.

THE KING AND QUEEN ON THE WIDE AUSTRALIAN PLAINS

AN EAST AFRICAN CAMP ON *SAFARI*

CHAPTER SIX

THE HANDICAPS OF HIS EARLY PUBLIC LIFE

IN the years of his youth the King was probably less concerned than any of his brothers in the attending of public functions in an official capacity or as a representative of Royalty. His sea service and his war experiences kept him fully occupied, and it was only when he was ashore and on leave that he was available for this kind of duty. Those opportunities were intermittent, and thus the public knew him less than they did the Duke of Windsor, but to-day with the increasing demand on the members of the Royal Family for their presence at celebrations and all official events the younger Princes were brought far more into the public eye. This modern version of the " fierce light that beats upon a throne " is one development of post-war days, one more manifestation of the People's love for their King and Princes and, in the alternative, the desire of Royalty to be as one with their people, sharing the same experiences and giving ungrudgingly all the service possible to their subjects.

Indeed, it is not until the war had finished that we begin to find any records of the King's public activities. He represented King George V—as has already been mentioned—at the formal entry of

the King of the Belgians into Brussels in November
1918, and was there again in February 1921 to present decorations to the famous Burgomaster Max
and the Prince de Croy. Other missions abroad of
these early post-war years were to Belgrade in 1922
and 1923, the first time to be " Koom " or sponsor
at the wedding of King Alexander of Serbia to Princess Marie of Rumania, and the second time (his
first tour on the Continent with Queen Elizabeth
after their marriage) when he again represented
King George V at the christening of Prince Peter,
the infant son of the Royal couple at whose wedding
he had been some sixteen months previously. In
between those visits was another to a Central European state, when he officiated for King George V
at the Coronation of the King and Queen of Rumania
at Bucharest in October 1922. At home he acted for
the King or for the Duke of Windsor at many functions, his year at Cambridge being much interrupted
by this sort of engagement.

There were, moreover, two very serious reasons
apart from his naval service and University reading
which had handicapped him throughout his life,
and kept him of necessity somewhat in the background. These handicaps were both physical and
both severe. One was the very obstinate gastric
trouble, which developed soon after he went to
Osborne, and the other his hesitancy of speech
which had been with him all his life. The gastric
trouble, after harassing all his boyhood years, keeping him out of many months of sport and pleasure,

and affecting all his studies, was cured after two very grave operations—one for appendicitis and the other for duodenal ulcer, as the illness was finally and correctly diagnosed. Those operations, as has been mentioned, prevented him from carrying on continuous war service in *Collingwood*, but as the King himself admits, it may have been good for him in another way. With a constitution weakened by his successive bouts of pain and his months of suffering, it is doubtful whether the rigours of winter service afloat, under war conditions and with food of war-time quality and quantity, would not have found him incapable of resisting the inroads of the disease resulting either in death or permanent invalidism. Even as it was the operations, their causes and their effects, left him delicate for a considerable period, and he had to be very careful of himself at all times for quite a long period after the second operation had " short-circuited " the ulcer.

His other handicap remained for a few years longer. The defect was even more obstinate than the gastric trouble had been. The shyness and diffidence which marked him as a boy were undoubtedly aggravated by the fear that he might not be able to begin a sentence, or having begun it, might not be able to finish it. The effect on a small retiring lad can be imagined. He tells himself of one incident at Dartmouth which, as boyish troubles will do, darkened many weeks of his first term there. His tutor, not knowing then the seriousness of his defect, asked him suddenly in class what was the half of a half. The King, nervous as a new boy can be, simply could not answer ; his speech, he said, froze in his throat. Thoroughly scornful, the tutor sarcastically deplored the backwardness of a boy who could not solve so simple a sum, and the King sat and blushed and wished the floor would open and swallow him. Nothing seemed to do him any good, though the best advice was sought and many systems tried. To speak in public was a bitter trial ; even to carry on a private conversation had its terrors. It speaks volumes for his high ideal of public duty and his own determination of character that in spite of what must have been recurrent mental agony to him he pursued his course bravely. One who knew him closely in those days tells of bouts of despair when, after a particularly bad time before a crowded roomful, or an audience of many thousands, he would sit for hours in deep gloom, wondering and doubting whether he would ever be any good. " I thought him then," his friend said, " one of the bravest men I knew, for always he got up, squared his shoulders and reiterated his determination to carry through." Indeed, everybody who came in contact with him in those years deeply admired the grit he displayed in fighting through in circumstances that would justifiably have deterred a weaker man and have given every excuse for the King himself to seek a life of semi-retirement in which the pain of constant hesitancy would have been reduced to a minimum. Instead, he chose the part of a determined man, never shirking his responsibilities, even seeking to take others on his shoulders and meeting the extra work entailed by the absences of the Duke of Windsor from England with a cheerful willingness to fill the breach to the very best of his ability.

Those were the days when system after system of speech training and voice production were tried, specialist after specialist consulted. All without success. The root mistake in all these futile courses was that the specialists assumed that the defect was due to nervousness—a mental condition. Naturally the King accepted that diagnosis, and this very knowledge (though erroneous), by reacting on his own inherent misgivings, only served to make matters worse for him. Nothing seemed to be of any use at all and the only policy, short of retiring from public life altogether—and that to the King was unthinkable—was to see that measures should be taken to cover up the defect as much as possible and practise extreme care in all directions which might alleviate the trial. Thus, for instance, great care was taken in the preparation of his speeches to choose such words and such words only as were comparatively easy for him to pronounce. One of the letters he found exceptionally difficult to speak was the hard guttural " K " sound. The same cause which prevented him from answering " a quarter " to the Dartmouth tutor prevented him always from referring to " the King," and in consequence he saw to it that in his speeches he always spoke of " His Majesty," if indeed, as he did frequently, he did not drop formality altogether and speak of him, delightfully, as " My father."

But all these measures were in reality mere manœuvres affecting only the fringe of the trouble and leaving the fundamental difficulties untouched. Things came to a head, however, when the King took over from the Duke of Windsor the Presidency of the Wembley Exhibition in 1925, and, with his brother away from England, found his public duties in connection with that great Empire project, and also in many other directions, increased more than twofold. Those months must have been a veritable nightmare to him, relieved on one occasion by a humorous incident which to-day, with all the trouble happily behind him, brings a reminiscent chuckle to his lips. He had to open the second year of the Exhibition before his father, in a set speech—an ordeal even for a practised speaker to stand in the centre of that huge Wembley arena, and depend on amplifiers for the voice to be carried to the audience. To anyone suffering from a speech defect the conditions were nerve shattering. But the King " got his laugh out of it," as the theatre comedian would say. The whole function had, of course, to be carefully rehearsed and the King attended the previous day to go through his part of the programme. When the time came to test the amplifiers the King stood up and began to speak into the microphones. But the switch had not been thrown on and no sound came through. The King turned to comment on the fact to the officials, when a mighty roar filled the

Stadium. "The damned things aren't working," it vociferated in the King's own voice, the engineers having chosen that very inconvenient moment to turn on the current!

Through the trials and tribulations of that year the King went gamely on, but it was becoming increasingly manifest that very drastic steps would have to be taken if he were not to develop into the shy, retiring, nervous individual which is the common fate of all those suffering from speech defects. His utterances, painful as they were sometimes to listen to, must have been trebly painful to deliver, but for the whole of 1925 and most of 1926 the King, to use his own words, "struggled through." Then came the announcement that he was to go to Australia with Queen Elizabeth to open the new Commonwealth Parliament House at Canberra. A world tour was planned in the battle-cruiser *Renown*, and it was certain that the whole of the six months away were going to be full of hard work for which the King would have to be physically "at his top" and not be continually on the tenter-hooks of apprehension lest his speech should fail him at most critical moments. The search for remedial measures therefore became intensified, and they even contemplated sending to the United States for a specialist who had recently come into prominence there as a curer of speech defects. Then one day when all were at their wits' end to know what to do, the King came into contact with the work of Mr. Lionel Logue, a specialist in speech defect, who had only recently arrived from Perth, West Australia, and had begun to practice in Harley Street. He was approached, and after a consultation, Mr. Logue became certain that the trouble was purely physical and not mental and should yield to the treatment he had spent many years of his life in perfecting.

That day—October 19th, 1926—meant much to the King. "He entered my consulting room," says Mr. Logue, "at three o'clock in the afternoon, a slim, quiet man, with tired eyes, and all the outward symptoms of the man upon whom habitual speech defect had begun to set the sign. When he left, at five o'clock, you could see that there was hope once more in his heart." He agreed to put himself unreservedly into Mr. Logue's hands, and it was expressly stipulated that he was to be treated in all things as an ordinary patient. Then began for the King one of the most strenuous periods of his life, for besides the multifarious duties he was daily called upon to perform, he had to attend at either the consulting rooms in Harley Street or Mr. Logue's house for an hour's closely concentrated work every day. More than that, in every spare moment he could get he had to exercise and practise according to the schedule mapped out for him by Mr. Logue. The one great advantage of that first consultation was that it had given the King assurance that he could be cured. Disillusioned so often before, the change in the outlook caused by the discovery that his trouble was physical and not as he had always feared, mental, re-established his confidence and renewed his determination. He plunged into the new work with enthusiasm. He realized that it meant making many sacrifices of his scanty leisure, many curtailments of his sport and pleasure. But he felt for the first time in his life that he was really on the road to recovery, and worked with energy and cheerfulness at whatever the routine of the day might happen to be. Even when out hunting in the middle of a glorious run, he would pull out of the field when the time came, hurry back to London and put in an hour's hard work before dinner. If his lot was work instead of play he always saw to it that the time-table of his day's engagements provided the necessary break somewhere so that he might fit in his " lesson " or his practice.

It was not long before results, most encouraging results, began to show. Certain sounds, difficult consonants, which before had meant a break in the continuity of the speech, began to be conquered and, with revived hope and energy, the Duke threw himself still more vigorously into the work. There was a big test for him before he left for Australia. The Pilgrims, perhaps more than any other dining-club accustomed to hearing the very best speakers in the world, were to give him a dinner as a farewell before departure. It was to be a memorable occasion with the late Lord Balfour in the chair and some of the best speakers in England on the toast list—an ordeal to try the most accomplished orator. The

King set his teeth and went for the job in hand as he has always done. His speech was prepared and revised by himself, and on the day of the banquet he left the hunting field early for a final rehearsal before going on to what he regarded as one of his biggest ordeals as a public speaker. Those who were at that dinner will not easily forget the surprise in store for them. They had expected a few hesitating words, a sentiment or two carefully phrased and very meticulously spoken. Instead, they found themselves listening to a smiling, almost fluent speaker, perhaps not yet speaking with the ease that the future brought to him, but with a conviction and a confidence most refreshing to hear. It was a revelation and the tables were quick to respond to the evident pleasure the King displayed in his new-found accomplishment. Afterwards he himself confessed—nobody knew it before—that he had taken the opportunity as a real test of his progress, and when he so triumphantly came through he felt it was the turning-point in his career and that really at last his handicap was fading into the past.

A very full schedule of study work and exercises was prepared for the King before he left for Australia, sufficient to fill in adequately every day of the six months' cruise. To that schedule the King applied himself with unremitting energy. In the midst of a most strenuous time of travel, under the tropic sun when everybody else on board was quite content to confine themselves to the minimum of brain work, he laboured faithfully at his self-appointed task. He reaped full reward, full and deserved reward. Among those who listened to the smooth delivery and well-expressed sentiments of his speech at the banquet the Commonwealth Government tendered him in Melbourne, or to the resonant quality of the voice that rang through the open air from the steps of Parliament House at Canberra, were many who had heard him at Wembley two years before. They were amazed at the difference, hardly believable, in the manner of diction and freedom from hesitancy which the King displayed. Some of them had met him and talked with him as President of the Exhibition. They remembered him as a silent, rarely smiling, reserved man, with an underlying charm of manner that would not be altogether denied expression, but still a man standing under the shadow of one of the most soul-destroying afflictions that can be imagined—a deep and obstinate speech defect. When they met him again in Australia, they found a happy smiling boyish Prince sure of himself, keen and eager to talk and get to the heart of things, learn everything for himself by question and answer—a different being altogether. And great as was the pleasure they found in this metamorphosis, it was eclipsed by the pleasure of the fortunate few who were associated with him on occasions when he was off duty, so to speak, and could let himself go without troubling the conventions. One such occasion lives and will live for ever in the memory of those who were lucky enough to be there. It was at Christchurch, after a day of popular enthusiasm seldom equalled and never exceeded throughout the tour. He had set aside the evening for a series of smoke concerts organized by the various Returned Soldiers' Organizations. The returned soldiers were of all grades, from the New Zealand Commander-in-Chief to the private who had scarcely made the front before the war was over. At the concerts he was not a King's son engaged on a high Imperial mission. He was just " one of the boys " and as keenly out for enjoyment as any of them. They made him a " Digger "; they cheered him on every possible occasion, they told stories that were certainly not meant for the drawing-room, and they sang the old trench songs in the veritable trench language. It was a genuine treat to see how the King reacted to it all. He laughed at all the jokes, sang the choruses of all the songs, and finally made one of the longest extempore speeches of his tour. For half an hour he spoke to his delighted audience without a note, and without a trace of hesitation in his utterance. More than that, his lack of self-consciousness was enough to allow him to answer the interjections which were hurled at him in the best possible spirit—and spirits—throughout. He countered them neatly too, so that the interjectors were still further encouraged to go on. That was the most notable extempore speech he made, though there were many others, particularly one at the close of the visit to Dunedin, where he again spoke for half an hour, this time in more serious vein and just as fluently. Always his continued ease and improving fluency were noticeable.

Just as soon as he arrived back in London, the King set to work again with Mr. Logue. He gave abundant proof that his improvement was permanent when at the Mansion House lunch at which the City welcomed the King and Queen Elizabeth back he spoke for half an hour pleasantly, smoothly, and with great charm, outlining the incidents of the tour and his hopes for the Empire he had so recently surveyed. Since then he has, according to Mr. Logue, under whose care he has ever since been, gone on from inprovement to improvement and sees within measurable distance the realization of another of his ambitions—to become a really first-class speaker. He thoroughly merits all this success. " The outstanding feature of the years he has spent with me," says Mr. Logue, " is the enormous capacity for work His Majesty possesses. When he first began to improve, he visualized what perfect speech was and nothing short of that ideal is going to satisfy him. For two years he never missed an appointment with me—a record of which he can with justice be proud. He realized that the will to be cured was not enough but that it called for grit, hard work, and self-sacrifice, all of which he gave ungrudgingly. Now he is ' come to his kingdom ' of content and confidence in diction."

The King pays enthusiastic tribute to his wife who, throughout the hard work of his earlier endeavours, was of inestimable assistance, her co-operation and encouragement spurring the King on to ever-renewed effort. There was one little incident of their newly married life which charmed all who saw it, even though it left a lump in the throat. At some lunch (the occasion is immaterial), the King and Queen Elizabeth were sitting together, and when the King rose to speak it was realized that his hesitancy was more than ever pronounced that day. The guests watched the struggle to articulate—and at times it was a real physical effort to get a word out—with ever-deepening sympathy. And then, when it seemed as though the King must give up the unequal fight and sit down with his speech undelivered, they saw the bride's hand steal out and up to grasp the King's fingers with a little reassuring pressure as though to give him encouragement to go on. He did.

CHAPTER SEVEN

TOUR OF EAST AFRICA

IT was not until the year 1924 that the King followed in the footsteps of his elder brother and began that very thorough journeying through the British Empire which has endeared both himself and the Queen to millions of the subjects of the British Empire. It had been King George's dearest wish that his sons should go and see for themselves, and just as soon as the war ended that wish was gratified, first by his eldest son the Duke of Windsor, then by the King, and in succession by Prince Henry Duke of Gloucester and Prince George Duke of Kent. All of them now have seen a goodly portion of the earth's surface; all of them are steadily enlarging their acquaintance and deepening their experiences in the best way calculated to cement the bonds of Empire, if one may use in its most adequate sense a phrase rather shop-worn by perfervid Imperial orators. There had been in the case of the King a few previous voyages and sojourns in various parts of the Empire, but it is hardly reasonable to take into consideration in this category the trip of instruction he made as a cadet in H.M.S. *Cumberland*, though the enthusiasm which his visit everywhere created was heartfelt, or the round of visits he paid to Northern Ireland with the Queen in July of 1924.

So that we may consider the East African tour he made at the end of 1924 and the beginning of 1925 as the true beginning of his real " Imperial " career —a kind of preliminary canter so to speak, heralding the Imperial Odyssey he was to undertake two years later. His first penetration of the outer marches was a very unpretentious one, " quite an ordinary private visit " as he has described it, and in no way so exacting as the Australian tour of 1927 in the matter of official functions and ceremonial. The King and Queen Elizabeth booked as ordinary passengers on the liner *Mulbera*, leaving Marseilles on December 8th, and their staff was cut down to the smallest dimensions —Rear-Admiral Sir Basil Brooke and Lieutenant-Commander Colin Buist in attendance on the King, and Lady Annaly as Lady-in-Waiting to the Queen. Winter-time gave them a bearable Red Sea passage, and soon after leaving Aden the King met Neptune across the line, for despite his sea career he had never been far enough south before to take a ducking. Still, he went fairly close to that dangerous zone when on the *Cumberland* cruise. He was shaved and dosed and ducked all in traditional style, and it is painful to have to chronicle that Neptune " double crossed him " over the affair. For when *Renown* crossed the line on the voyage to New Zealand, in 1927, the Lord of the Sea refused to accept the King's prior initiation and insisted that as he had only been entered from the deck of a passenger ship

ON THEIR WAY HOME FROM EAST AFRICA

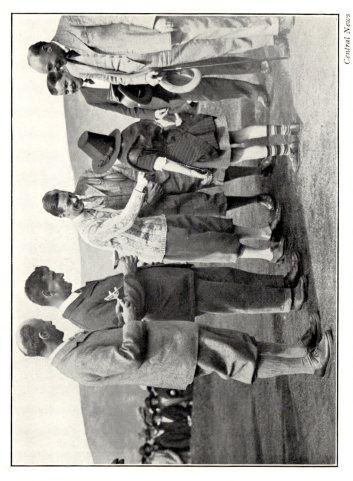

THE YOUNGER GENERATION DOES HER DUTY

such an insignificant ceremonial could not be recognized. So the King was admitted to the order of sea dogs once again, while the Queen, as she had done before, looked delightedly on at the proceedings.

The King and Queen Elizabeth arrived at Mombasa on December 21st. The Governor of Kenya, the late Sir Robert Coryndon, met them on board and took them ashore for the inevitable lunch and garden party to introduce them to the British colonists and also to give them their first taste of native custom and ceremonial with a " ngoma " or native dance, the first in an already long list of primitive corybantics which the King and Queen Elizabeth have seen in all parts of the world and in all manner of strange surroundings. Such, for example, as the weird " pig-dance " before the Resident's house in lonely Nukuhiva, one of the Marquesas Islands, where decorously dressed Polynesians danced under kerosene flares to the music of drums made of petrol tins. Or the queer combination of old and new at Rotorua in New Zealand, when a few Poi dancers swung their anciently fashioned flax balls on a modern stage in front of the conventional wings and backcloth. Or again, the Aboriginal corroboree in Queensland, a relic of a day that was far older in point of time than either of the "civilizations" already mentioned. There is indeed a whole chapter to be written on their experiences alone in this direction.

The stay in Mombasa was necessarily brief, for they had to leave the same afternoon for Nairobi, the capital of the colony, situate on the more salubrious uplands of the interior. Avid for new sensation and fresh experiences, the King and Queen rode for part of the railway journey on a specially constructed platform in front of the engine so that they might see the vista of the lush tropical vegetation of the littoral change to the forest-clad slopes of the inland plateau, and gain their first sight unobstructed by saloon windows of the teeming animal life of the colony. What they saw made them all the more eager to be up and off to the hunting-grounds, and they gave to Nairobi only the few days devoted to the Christmas festivities before betaking themselves to their first hunting camp at Siola on the opening days of the New Year.

It was while at this camp that the King had his first thrill of big-game hunting. He and the White Hunter were out walking when they followed the trail of two rhinoceroses into long grass and through some very thick bush. They came upon them quite suddenly in an open space at a distance of about eight yards or so. Surprised at the appearance of the two strange-looking humans, the rhinos, to use the King's own modest description of the incident, got up to run away. One of them as he rose faced the King and the White Hunter at very close quarters, and was immediately shot, while his companion escaped. There was a most amusing sequel to this incident. A very sensational account of the affair appeared in a London paper, the outcome of the enterprise of its local correspondent. Delays in cabling and so on made it seem as though the incident had occurred on Sunday, and a rigid Sabbath Observance organization raised the customary objection to hunting on the Lord's Day. The King's reply to the private cable of inquiry that was sent to him was that in the first place the incident had not happened on a Sunday, in the second that he had not shot a rhinoceros, and in the third that he would never be sure that rhinoceroses knew when it was Sunday. A little later on he was to get a positive " charge." The White Hunter and himself walked up a lioness and she charged from about thirty yards. The two rifles spoke together and she dropped about fifteen yards away.

All through the month of January the party was either changing camp or shooting over a wide extent of country. The Queen was as keen on the chase as the King, and together they accumulated a fine collection of good heads as specimens of the teeming wild life of Kenya. They lived in those days the rough life of the ordinary seeker after game, and few nights were spent in the same place or under the same kind of roof. Usually it was a canvas tent, set and struck with all the military exactitude that is so easily taught to native forces, but sometimes it was a mud house of curious design that had been prepared for them. Always there was the chance that a violent wind would carry away the whole of their night's coverings or that a sudden torrential downpour would wash them out of their beds. These and other incidents almost as exciting were their daily, or perhaps nightly, portion, while their days were filled with the strong draughts of life as it is lived in the outposts of Empire and the thrill of pitting their wits against the creatures of the wild.

All things, however, have to come to an end, and with the approach of February the King and Queen had to return to civilization as it is known in Nairobi —and there the people do understand the amenities of semi-tropical existence—to prepare for their homeward journey through Uganda and down the Nile. They left on that journey on February 7th, but only three days later the Governor died very sadly and suddenly, and the King hurried back to Nairobi in order to be present at the funeral. Again " on the march," the party made for the northern end of Victoria Nyanza, where they took ship in a lake steamer to cross to the other side. They made a detour on the voyage to Jinjja that they might see the Ripon Falls, usually regarded as the source of the Nile, upon which river they were so soon to spend many days. The country to which they were going was different from the one they had left. Wilder, more remote than ever from the coast, its people compact of many tribes kin only in one thing, and that, their tribal pride and fierce nation- alism. The last century was in its second half while they were still pagan, still primitive, still warlike. They paid loyalty to feudal chiefs, they exacted tribute on their behalf—or their own—from weaker brethren, and they fought cheerfully and to the death at the bidding of their feudal lords. Even the name was unknown eighty years ago. Then a party of trading Arabs from the coast found a tribe at the head of Lake Victoria who had established a temporary supremacy over the other tribes in the territory. This tribe called themselves the Baganda, but being evidently attached to the suffix, they called their country Buganda, while their language was Luganda and the generic term for an individual of the tribe was Muganda. Accepting the predominant suffix, the Arabs labelled the whole of the new trading centre, its people and its patois, Uganda, and thus the name was born. The Baganda are again the paramount tribe of Uganda, their chief, " the Kabaka," the paramount chief. There are four other districts, though, with their own chiefs who owe no direct allegiance or homage to the Kabaka—in that sense there is no King of Uganda, though there are kings in Uganda.

It is due to the present Kabaka that Uganda has to-day emerged so far upon the path of progress, though it was his grandfather, the famous Mtesa or Mutesa, who first opened his country to missionary zeal in religious education while he himself remained a pagan. But his son Mwanga let the country slip back far into the horror and the bloodshed of the bad old days. His despotic and terrible rule brought the interference of the British in the interests of civilization, and Mwanga agreed to the establishment of a British Protectorate in 1893. Old habits were too ingrained, however, and in 1899 he was exiled to the Seychelles. That ended the period of misrule. His son, now His

Highness Sir Daudi Chwa, K.C.M.G., who had succeeded his father in 1897, had had an English education and had renounced paganism for Christianity. But his days in England had invested him with a tolerance which found expression during the many years of his beneficent rule in the re-establishment of the idea of feudalism coupled with the ideal of a paternal government. Those twin ambitions the British administrators did their best to foster. They preserved the Kabaka and his fellow-kings in their allotted majesty, acting towards them the part of beneficent and more or less disinterested advisers, and using the existing social system as a base upon which to found the very efficient administration Uganda enjoys to-day.

It was to this country, fascinating in its combination of the very old and the very new, that the King and Queen came in the middle of February. A huge flotilla of war canoes met their lake steamer some miles out on the waters of the Victoria Nyanza. Manned by stalwart Baganda, crammed to the gunwale with warriors in all the barbaric splendour of their fighting garb, the steamer swept to the landing-stage in a kaleidoscopic weaving of swiftly moving craft. The Royal party landed at Entebbe, the official and administrative centre of Uganda, the Canberra of the territory, so to speak. There, on high ground in the middle of a vast park overlooking the lake, stands Government House and many of the Government departments. The park lands are laid out as a botanic garden, and in all respects it has a perfect setting. The following day it was the turn of the native capital Kampala (Mengo), which is to-day also the business, educational, and religious centre. Set on Seven Hills, it is very excellently laid out, the old haphazard planning of the native town having given way to wide streets, under police control of traffic—" Point duty on the Equator "—could anything more emphasize the English habit of creating a home from home ? On the crest of one of the hills stood Lugard's fort, its place taken to-day by the very modern villa of the Indian merchant who made a a fortune by selling Coventry-made bicycles to prosperous natives. Two other summits carry the English Cathedral and the Roman Catholic mission. Near at hand is the Makerere College, the coping-stone of the very enlightened educational system of Uganda, which began with the devoted teaching of the missionaries whom Mtesa allowed to guide his pagan subjects on towards higher things. There native students who have distinguished themselves in the elementary and secondary schools may carry their learning further and fit themselves for teaching, medicine, and veterinary work, agriculture, engineering, and clerical training. So that as the years pass the Government departments are being increasingly staffed by the natives themselves, while those of the students who elect to go back to their own towns will carry there the instruction in the amenities of sanitary and personal hygiene which will mean so much to the future health and well-being of the race.

At Kampala the Kabaka, whose palace stands upon another of the Seven Hills, received the King and Queen and presented them with many gifts. There, too, he accorded them the compliment of a magnificent Omoleko, or military review—the finest that had been held for years. Chosen from all parts of the territory, the lines of tall natives in full war regalia marched past the saluting post, shouting their tribal cries, breaking into their peculiar war steps as they approached the base. Of special interest were the native drums which throbbed out the marching tunes, led by the King's own great drums, the Majauzu, only used on special state occasions. Those drums had in past ages stirred to wild excesses the blood-drunken Baganda of the old unhappy days. To-day their mission is as innocuous as the Guards' Band on the Whitehall parade ground. The next day the King and Queen were to see a more peaceful manifestation of the way in which the new ideas have been grafted on to the old customs—and incidentally to have a demonstration of the excellent roads the administration have driven through the length and breadth of the land. They motored more than two hundred miles to Fort Portal, there to visit a Lukiko or native parliament. These parliaments are the method employed in the various districts to settle native problems and savour a good deal in procedure of the old Saxon Witenagemot. The King's visit to the Lukiko was made the occasion for a display of complicated native ceremonial by the crowds of white-clad Baganda and the native orchestras which accompanied the proceedings with reeds and tom-toms, varying the programme with long recitals of the ruler's many virtues or the transcendent qualities of the Royal visitors. Many were the loyal addresses presented and great was the enthusiasm. The members of these Lukikos discuss gravely all manner of native affairs, such as the matter of cotton regulations or the question of inheritance of native lands. There is the right to appeal to higher courts, but generally the system works very well and the natives are naturally anxious to take a part in their own government.

From Fort Portal the party dropped down the steep escarpment into the Semliki valley, where it is said the hunters of King Solomon once gathered " ivory and apes and peacocks " for the Queen of Sheba. The party walked down the steep trails to the lower levels, where they marched and hunted by day until the trek ended on the shores of Lake Albert at a little sand-baked port, Butiaba, where they embarked on board the *Samuel Baker*, a shallow-draught steamer drawing only four feet, which could—and did—roll in the swell that swept across the wide levels of the lake. In her they crossed to the northern end of the lake and debouched into the Bahr el Jebel, the White Nile, which is the overflow of the Albert Nyanza. They were still in the highlands of the interior, with cool weather and a panorama of broken scenery which must have reminded them both of Scotland, except where the river broadened out occasionally into wide areas of the typical Nile Sudd, of which they were to see later such interminable miles and miles. They steamed down the White Nile for two days, landing and embarking passengers and goods, cotton and ivory, specimens from hunting parties, hides, and timber for fuel, while they watched from the deck crocodiles and hippos sunning themselves on sand bars or sinking lazily out of sight as the steamer approached. At the end of the voyage in the *Samuel Baker* they came to Nimule, the port which marks the boundary between Uganda and the Sudan. From there the river enters upon a hundred miles of turbulent water, waterfalls and cascades, rapids and whirlpools, swamps and shallows which take it from the broken country of the plateau to the dead flat levels of the Nile Valley proper. It is not navigable, never can be, and it required a hundred miles of motoring before the King and Queen could reach Rejaf, the station on the upper river where the real Nile navigation begins. And here one cannot resist quoting from an article in the London *Daily Telegraph* by Mr. Owen Tweedy, who made the same journey in an opposite direction a little before them. Leaving Rejaf—

" The green flatness of the Nile valley had changed into parched undulating grasslands now studded untidily with stunted flat-topped trees, now broken by wide valley bottoms of red sand and hill slopes of black volcanic rock. The monotony of the limitless horizons to the north was replaced by long vistas of hills, carpeted with pale yellow scrub grass, and slabbed with red rock buttresses and gorse-like patches of thorn. Perfect piccaninnies with shining pot-bellies capered and screamed and vied among themselves to throw a ' Guards ' salute. Women wearing a string of beads from which hung in front an apology of a fringe and behind a vivid green tuft of leaves swayed ample Parisian figures of the 'nineties in contortions of laughter and screaming. The men lolled in boredom upon their spears—for all the world the personification of male superiority. All were jet black, all practically naked, all unself-conscious and unashamed. Some say the Garden of Eden was in Africa."

For five weeks after leaving Rejaf on the comfortable *Nasir* the party travelled north, steaming by day and camping ashore for a spell where the locality promised good sport. The wide reaches of the river flowing implacably northward have a grandeur all their own, but the almost unrelieved level of the banks tends to become monotonous. Through a territory that stretched for nearly a thousand miles down-stream the *Nasir* plugged northward, only occasionally making a stop—because in that vast area of riverine marsh known as the Sudd only a few stops are practicable. But, although they saw comparatively few humans, the party had many indications that the southern Sudan away from the inhospitable river marshes did support a teeming population, and when more opened up by railways and enriched by irrigation could support millions more. At Tonga, for example, they left the river and motored into the hills that fringed the Nile valley to see a splendid march past of twelve thousand Nubian warriors, followed by a hair-raising display of spear throwing as well as wrestling and dancing. Later on again at Kodok—which is the modern Fashoda—the natives staged a most realistic sham-fight for them, " darkening the air with their assegais," and going through a complete programme of their war games for their special benefit.

At Kosti they landed again for a very different experience—to see a demonstration of what the Sudan administration was doing for the development of the vast province and the betterment of the conditions of the millions of natives of many tribes and tongues which inhabit the area. They entrained for Sennar, there to see the mighty dam across the upper waters of the Blue Nile holding back a huge volume of water for the irrigation of hundreds of thousands of acres of cotton-growing country, already showing in the increasing cotton exports of the Sudan the result of the enlightened ideals which were responsible for its building. The next day, April 7th, they were in civilization again at Khartoum, where they were welcomed by thousands of all nationalities, and a few days later the King and Queen left Port Sudan for home.

As he himself said on his return, the King came back to England profoundly impressed by all he had seen in these newer territories of his native land.

He had seen in Kenya the best type of Britons following in the footsteps of the pioneers and missionaries,
but striving to make life in that subtropical depen-
dency as closely conforming to the perfect conditions
of English country-house life as could be. He had
seen cheek by jowl, not once, but a dozen times, a
native grass hut and, rising into the shimmering air
of the warm uplands, the walls and chimneys of a
faithfully reproduced Jacobean manor or a seaside
villa. He had met and talked with men whose
fathers were primitive pagans, but who, themselves,
were courteous, well-spoken, well-educated men of
affairs, the result of only fifty years of English contact
and administration. He had seen all manner of
men and women from the scion of British aristocracy
carving out a coffee or banana plantation for himself
from the primeval forest, to a Congo pigmy in the
Semlik valley. He had rubbed shoulders with
thousands of African natives—Baganda, Arabs,
Nuers, Nubians, Dinkas—of all grades of culture
from the most primitive to the Western educated.
Over and above all he was deeply impressed by the
way in which the English—and the Scotch—of the
various administrations were carrying on their work.
Youngsters, for the most part far removed from
headquarters, shouldering their myriad responsibilities cheerfully and adequately, winning the confidence of their districts by their straight dealing and
sound common sense, the high traditions of their
calling and their appreciation of the native view-
point. It is an old story, told any time since the

English began to colonize. It is a story that breaks with a new light, a new significance upon every traveller—as it came home to the King again in those crowded months of new sights, new sounds, new knowledge, and new pride in the Empire of which he was a part.

CHAPTER EIGHT

THE YOUNGER GENERATION

ALMOST as soon as the King began to take his full share of the duties of Royalty—sometimes more than his full share—he developed a very deep and abiding ideal, which has stayed with him all through the years. He wants with a sincerity almost amounting to a passion to help in every way and with all his heart in the improvement of the bodily condition and mental health of the individual.

> " Not the great nor well bespoke
> But the mere uncounted folk."

In the pursuance of that ideal he begins with the individual practically in the cradle. Of the thousands of photographs that have been taken of him in many hundreds of scenes, not the least touching are those which portray him leaning over a cot in a children's hospital, or with his Queen talking to an obstreperous pair of twins in a perambulator. There is a gleam of sympathy, of very real humanity in his face then, which even the flatness of a photograph or the mechanical changes made during the preparation of a three-tone engraving cannot wholly destroy. It would be the commonplace thing to say that this

95

tenderness for the child is inspired by his devotion to his own much-loved daughters—and doubtless the arrival in this world of those daughters has had much to do with the wider understanding and broader outlook on the children's kingdom he now displays.

But the root of his ideal lies deeper and more firmly based even than that. It springs from a solidly founded conviction that the might of the Empire and its future lie in the lap of the younger generation now growing up towards their responsibilities as citizens. He sees no bounds to that responsibility, no lessening of its requirements in any grade of life. To him the waif of the city slum is just as important as the public-schoolboy. Their function is the same, though their methods of attaining it may differ. To help them to that attainment is, it may be said without contradiction, the King's dearest desire. Show him at any time any way in which he may help, and you have immediately a fervent worker in the particular field that has been indicated to him. He is never too busy, too preoccupied with other affairs that he cannot lay them aside to discuss a new betterment plan, to listen to some fresh development in welfare work, which his ardent band of advisers may place before him, to offer not only sympathy but also valuable suggestions as to the most efficacious way of carrying out the plans. This facet of his public life began practically when the life itself began. In the year after the war he became president

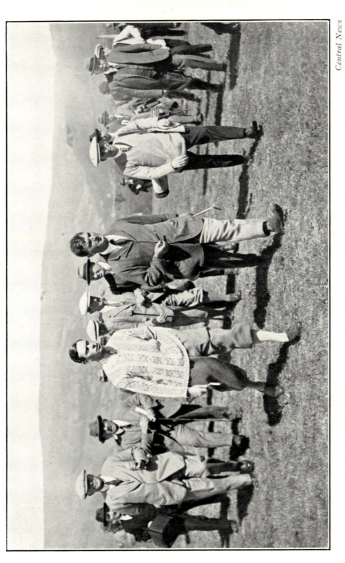

PLAYING GOLF WITH MR. FRANK HODGES DURING A WELFARE TOUR

Central News

DRIVING THE GLASGOW TRAM

of the Boys' Welfare Society, an organization later to develop into something of much further reaching importance—the Industrial Welfare Society. But while still a separate entity the Boys' Welfare Society provided the stimulus and the avenue alike wherein the King could expand and extend his chosen aims and objects. The contacts he made then with the lives of boys and youths in the working areas of Great Britain, the insight that contact gave him into the homes and living conditions of those boys who were soon to become the workers of the community, and whose fathers had done their bit in the saving of the Empire, were to him a revelation. What he learnt then stirred his blood and quickened his senses as no other method of investigation could have done, and from that first year he has never wearied in well-doing and in the encouragement by every means in his power of all efforts to brighten the lives and broaden the outlook of the children and the youth of these Dominions. But even more than the knowledge he gained from personal contact in those days there came to him a friendship, one might say an affection, for the youngsters who thronged round his car when he made his public visits, or cheered him shrilly when he passed through their districts on his way to public functions, or showed so unmistakably their appreciation when he had brought about something that made life more pleasant for them—from the securing of a school half-holiday to the opening of a new playing field for their benefit. It was this affection that prompted his disposal of the £2500 wedding gift which a section of the community had offered him on his marriage. He divided it into five equal parts and requested the Mayors of five of the principal towns in industrial areas to spend it on treats for children on his wedding day. It was through the same thoughtfulness that at his express desire twenty factory boys, drawn from the member firms of the Industrial Welfare Society, were specially invited to attend the wedding ceremony in Westminster Abbey.

Although in keenness this attitude of his never slackened from the first, it is probable that his Australasian tour enlarged and consolidated his affection and enthusiasm for the life of the child and the provision for its present welfare and future prosperity. As his first experiences with the Boys' Welfare Society had revealed to him conditions that pressed him towards greater effort in their behalf, so the tour widened his horizon in this regard and showed him, as nothing else could have done, in what great fields, under what splendid conditions, the weakly town-bred child of an English industrial town would become the hardy young sprig of bone and muscle he saw wherever he went. Both in New Zealand and in Australia the authorities saw to it that no opportunity was missed for the Royal visitors to see all the children of the community—and what was perhaps more important from their point of view, that all the children of the community should see them. From the opening of the tour at Auckland to its close at Perth, he saw child life and child enthusiasm under all manner of conditions, in all phases of life. Perhaps those two cities provided in themselves the epitome of his experiences. In the first he shared in, or rather he and the Queen were the central figures in, a very wonderful demonstration of youthful en- thusiasm which, while it gladdened the heart, must have brought emotion very close to the throat. The occasion was the children's demonstration in the Domain, the day a glorious one of sun and wind when the spirit of youth was everywhere abroad. Fifteen thousand school children from all the districts round Auckland and from the city itself had been assembled to go through a full programme of Swedish drill, Flag drill, and the many clever evolutions and marches which modern physical teaching has developed. There was no possible doubt as to the well-being of these youngsters. They glowed with health and excitement, shrilling their cheers with fortissimo effect, and in the end breaking all bounds of carefully inculcated discipline. When the demonstration was over the King and Queen gave instructions that their open car should make the circuit of the grounds, threading its way in and out of the long lines of children still standing decorously to attention. But who, in the full flush of youth, with rapturous excitement still bubbling, could possibly withstand the temptation of having a real live Prince and Princess down among them so close as almost to be touched ? Certainly not fifteen thousand high-spirited young Aucklanders. First a dozen or so broke ranks and followed the car, shouting their enthusiasm. Then scores, then hundreds, until at length the whole wide arena was one surging mass of almost hysterical children thronging about the car, shouting, cap waving, rushing excitedly from vantage point to vantage point, while the King and Queen stood in their car smiling, hand waving, and most evidently touched by the whole-souled worship of their younger subjects.

At Perth, when the tour was ending, there was an experience of quite a different nature, but one in its way even more symptomatic, more calculated to appeal to the King's ideal and establish his opinions still more firmly. A half-day's journey from Perth, at Pinjarra, there are the Fairbridge Farm Schools. The original of the foundations which will soon have their counterpart in other parts of His Majesty's Dominions overseas, the result of an idea backed by the burning zeal of one man—Kingsley Fairbridge, such a man as, if he had been alive to-day, the King would have delighted to honour, would have been proud and content to have worked alongside in the cause of the child. Kingsley Fairbridge spent an ordinary out-of-door childhood in South Africa and was an early Rhodes Scholar at Oxford. Like so many high-souled idealists he became involved in what was then known as settlement work. Down in the East End of London and in other of the slum centres he became hopeless, despairing of the future of the children doomed to be brought up in the squalor and wretchedness of their surroundings. He conceived the idea of relieving the pressure and the poverty of the slums, which had become a byword, by taking the small children away from the deadening surroundings and sending them out to the healthier, happier conditions they would meet in the newer countries of the South. Thus were the Fairbridge Farm Schools born to be, as they are to-day, a very valuable, very efficient scheme in the migration of the peoples of the Empire to places where the Empire wants people. As President of the Dr. Barnardo Homes, the King had seen many times, before he left London on his Australian tour, the first steps in that transformation which was to turn the pale-faced, under-nourished, sickly child of the slums into the brown-skinned rascal of the Sunny South. He was profoundly impressed by the contrast that awaited him in Pinjarra. There, under the kindly skies of Western Australia, the youngsters live under as free a control as could be evolved for the better moulding of their characters; from there they are drafted to farms and stations through the length and breadth of the State's broad acres, to become in their due time real Australians and real Empire builders, of worth to themselves and the country of their adoption, a credit to the country of their birth. The King has put on record more than once his abiding impression of that visit. "Never," he told an audience soon after his return, "have I seen such a healthy, happy group of children. Children transferred from the gutter and the street to the beauty and healthfulness of Australia will live to bless the name of Kingsley Fairbridge." The whole episode must have gone far to confirm him in the belief in the wisdom of the choice he had made in determining to devote himself to the fortunes of the younger generation.

Between the two events there had been a hundred other incidents to tighten still closer his resolve to go forward on the appointed path, or to drive home to him the high importance of the younger generation. There was the walk to the municipal pavilion at Palmerston in New Zealand, where the King and Queen, to please the youngsters, dismissed their car and passed to their dais the whole way between lines of children so that they might see them closer and know them better. There was his concern for the children at Greymouth, the West Coast mining town in New Zealand. As usual, a children's demonstration had been arranged. But it rained—not that the child of the West Coast minds rain any more than the child of the west coast of Ireland. Still, parading in the drizzle is always unpleasant, so the King insisted that the drill should be called off and the children housed in the local theatre, where he chatted to them unconventionally for an hour or so, and then upset the official ukase that they were not to be admitted to the railway platform to say good-bye. When the train drew out it left behind a thousand children of good mining stock who were convinced that they had a new hero to worship. Again, on the day of the departure from Sydney, in a storm of wind and rain, a ferry boat crammed with school children, heedless of the elements, drifted round *Renown*, the youngsters singing lustily against the gale. No wonder with events such as these, crowding each other's heels throughout the tour, the King coined the slogan :

" Take care of the children and the country will take care of itself."

He used it first in Wellington and several times afterwards. He has quoted it more than once since then. It appeals to him as embodying all his own ideal, all his own conviction on the question of child welfare.

An offshoot, so to speak, of his interest in children and all that pertains to their welfare is the King's position as Patron of the National Safety First Council, a body designed to encourage care in driving and in crossing the more and more traffic-congested roads of Great Britain. It seeks to further the policy of safety first by holding essay competitions in the schools and by seeing that teachers try to impress on their classes the necessity of exercising watchfulness in walking and playing. In large cities where playing-grounds are at a premium and the children have perforce to use the streets for their games, it is of the utmost importance that they should also be told over and

over again in as direct a manner as possible how
to preserve their life and limbs, and the Association
is doing very much good in this direction. An
incident in administration which occurred during
the early years of his being patron is useful as an
indication of the serious way in which the King
regards his responsibilities. More often than not
the gentlemen who have been honoured by selection
as Patrons are inclined to regard that position as
merely a sinecure, and to salve their conscience with
a yearly cheque. Not so the King. It happened that
he, in common with many members of the Association, thought that the title " Safety First " was in
some respects a misnomer, likely to convey a totally
wrong impression of the objects and ideals of the
organization. As one speaker at a discussion on
the question somewhat bluntly but nevertheless
directly put it, school children were more and more
coming to think that the motto meant : " Your
own safety first and be blowed to anyone else's."
The King was somewhat of the same opinion, and
therefore wrote to the executive a very clear expression of his opinion " That it cannot but be detri-
mental to retain a title which provokes criticism
on the grounds that it is not in accordance with
the British qualities of courage and sportsmanship."
He thought that a slight alteration might be desir-
able, but was, with his usual tact and understanding,
very careful to explain that he had no wish whatever
to impose his opinion on the executive, and made
it quite clear that his interest in and support of the

movement would in no way be affected by the decision of the members whatever that decision might be. The whole incident is just one of those many sidelights available that cast an illuminating gleam on the anxiety of the King to be of real help to any movement which may enlist his sympathy. As the outcome of discussion among members, the name still remains the same, but in another direction the King was responsible for the formation of an analogous body with a name far more descriptive of its objects. Speaking to a meeting of children when presenting the prizes for an essay competition, the King told his hearers : " Start early to cultivate a spirit of good fellowship on the road." This one remark inspired the giving to the road-users' section of the Association the name of " The Road Fellowship League," which perhaps more aptly indicates its ideal than " Safety First." On many other occasions, by his presence or his messages, the King has shown for the Association that genuine personal interest he takes in everything with which he allows his name to be connected. Whatever be his opinion of the Association's slogan, he believes in the principles, for as he said at one meeting, they " will go far to solve not only the accident problem but many other ills from which all nations are suffering, since by training people to think more deeply before they act you are helping to prevent accidents of other kinds than those which figure on your programme."

It may be that the facts he learnt through his

association with the " Safety First " campaign—
how grievous was the toll in death and injury levied
on the poor youngsters who found no playground
but the street and ran daily—hourly—momentary
risks from wheeled traffic in the pursuit of their
simple and hard-won pleasures—added enthusiasm
to the King's acceptance of the Presidency of the
National Playing Fields Association when that very
estimable organization was formed in 1925. He
accepted the position before the inaugural meeting
and forever after he has shown the keenest personal
interest in the movement, which has for its object
the provision of adequate playing fields for the four
or five million British children who at present have
no outlet for their energies but the public highways
with all their dangers. Though, as in most similar
cases of public appeal, the Association was, at
first and still is, hampered by lack of funds, it has
done and is doing an extraordinary amount of
excellent work, not only in the field of propaganda
but also in the more solid achievement of securing
open spaces for their objects. Under the scheme,
initiated in 1927, the grants for the establishment or
upkeep of playing fields made by the National
Playing Fields Association and the Carnegie Trust,
working in collaboration have approximated to
£300,000, and an additional £7000 from the King
George Jubilee Trust Fund has also been expended.
Ten times that amount will be needed for the
completion of the scheme for the country-wide
provision of playing fields. Further benefit will

accrue to the scheme from King George Memorial Fund, though, as the King, who became the Chairman of the Advisory Council, has more than once reminded the community, there remains much to be done before the growing generation, especially in the congested industrial areas, will have assigned to them sufficient playing fields, gymnasiums, and other outlets of healthy youth to keep them fit and well.

The King has spoken often in favour of the Association throughout the country. He has been of very real help to the executive in its discussion of schemes for the supply of either money or lands in furtherance of their objective. He has never failed to respond to any suggestion that may have come from them as to other ways in which he might help the movement. Even when he was still thousands of miles distant from Britain, returning from his world tour in *Renown*, he wirelessed a message from the middle of the Indian Ocean to inaugurate the appeal for funds for the scheme under which the Association is still working. He still maintains his keen interest in the whole effort, though his activity is more devoted to outside investigation and propaganda than in the internal management of the business. He will always ask to see what provision has been made for playing fields in whatever locality he may happen to be visiting, and there is no suggestion made for increased effort or wider missionary enterprise that does not find his ready response. Indeed, so closely has he become identified with the movement that already a crop of stories has gathered round his activities, one of the best of which he told himself to an audience. One morning two little chaps presented themselves at 145 Piccadilly and asked diffidently whether they could see the King. Questioned as to their mission, they explained that their usual pitch had been appropriated for some public purpose —and what was the King going to do about it, please? The King did something very quickly and very effectively. The L.C.C. was very sympathetic, and those boys were made happy for the rest of the summer with room to play the national game in surroundings that left them happier and healthier for all time.

This practical application of the *mens sana in corpore sano* idea by no means stops short with the boy or girl. Age is no bar to the enjoyment of the playing fields ; years do not, in reason, prevent participation in the pleasures of the open air. The twelve-year-old soon—too soon—finds himself outside the school age earning a livelihood, and no one would deny to him the sports he enjoyed in his schoolboy days. Not at any rate the National Playing Fields Association or the scores of local authorities who work under its stimulus, or the many organizations who have in their care and under their supervision the athletic needs of hundreds and thousands of factory lads and office workers. In that category, as in every other welfare effort, the King, as Duke of York, had his special interest, an interest that has a world-wide reputation, and is known throughout the length and breadth of the Empire as " The Duke of York's Camp." It may be said without reservation that it is the part of his public activities he enjoys the most whole-heartedly. Certainly in its absolute equality of association of all ranks it expresses alike in their highest form the democratic ideal and the King's own particular ambition to see that every one in the community without fear or favour should have a fair deal. Its origin is interesting. Soon after the war, when the Welfare Society had first begun its operations beyond the narrower limits of the Boys' Welfare Society which had merged into it, a party of young miners in South Wales had saved up enough money for a trip to London. The welfare worker of the district came with them and was anxious that they should play two or three football matches during the trip. He asked the Industrial Welfare Office in London to see whether this could be done. It was, and one of the matches so arranged was against Westminster School on the famous ground in Vincent Square, Westminster. The King, as President of the Welfare Society, was only too glad to meet these lads from Wales, and was so impressed by their general demeanour that he expressed a wish that something could be done on a bigger scale to bring about meetings between the public schools and working boys. Various schemes were submitted to him, and he seized on the idea of an annual camp as the best method of bringing them together under the most attractive surroundings.

An ideal site was found at New Romney, and the first camp—an unqualified success—was held there in 1921. The system has never been altered—there has never been any occasion for it to be. Boys from each of a hundred schools and boys from a hundred firms who are members of the Industrial Welfare Society are invited each year as the King's guests to the camp, and up to date nearly 6000 of them have passed through the annual camp and gone back to their ordinary life the richer by their knowledge of " the other man's " point of view. They are split into twenty sections of twenty boys, each of which contains ten public school boys and ten working boys. They sleep together, they mess together, do their camp " chores " together, acknowledge the control of a section leader to each section, and play together or in rivalry with other sections. It is all on a basis of perfect equality, and there has never since the camp started been any untoward incident to mar its happiness or heartiness. The King has only missed one year in visiting the camp since he started the scheme. That was in 1934 when a poisoned hand kept him away, and he has publicly stated on more than one occasion that it is the one day in the year to which he looks forward with undiluted pleasure. Certain it is on that day he abandons himself to all the outdoor delights of a lad in camp with every sign of thorough enjoyment. As soon as he arrives he hurries into shirt and shorts and strolls through the camp chatting with all and sundry, looking into their messing arrangements, inquiring as to their well-being, and interesting himself in the many activities of camp life. If there are any sports or games going on he joins in them, and there is a story told of one occasion when they had borrowed a push-ball from a neighbouring camp of Air Force men. Now push-ball is a very strenuous game, and the games leader, solicitous for the King's comfort, asked him to referee. " Referee be blowed," he replied, " I am going to play." Play he did. In the middle of the game, when both sides had their heads hard down to it, a young Rugger Blue was boring with his head into the ribs of a player in front of him. Giving him a tremendous butt, he shouted, " Go on, push like the devil ! " In a flash, the King's voice came out of the smother of backs and shoulders : " But I am pushing like the devil." It was his ribs that had been butted so generously.

Given fine weather, the day of the King's visit always ends with a sing-song round the camp fire, and there is no more lusty voice in the choruses or heartier laugh at the stories than his. It is over all too soon, for the pleasure not only of the King himself but of the boys who have had him with them all day. The day of his visit is always marked with a white stone, and many, very many, are the memories treasured in numberless homes of the cheery word or the slap on the back or the shout of encouragement that came to the lads from their host. " Why," said one of them one day in the King's hearing, " he's really a human being." That estimate is quoted with gusto by the King. Perhaps he is prouder of it than of many of the measured phrases of eloquent speakers to whom he has listened while they sing his praises. It sums up so succinctly just what he wants to be thought, just what he expects everybody to be when they come into contact with him.

CROSSING THE LINE

FISHING AT TOKAANU (NEW ZEALAND)

CHAPTER NINE

INDUSTRIAL WELFARE WORK

FROM the child to the boy, from the boy to the man. The King's interest and enthusiasm for the health of the child and the well-being of the boy are but manifestations of his all-embracing zeal for the welfare of every individual in the community. That zeal and that enthusiasm found their early outlet in his presidency of the Industrial Welfare Society, a position he has occupied ever since its inception as one of the good things which came out of the war. A few words as to its origin may not be amiss. During the war the unprecedented demand for munitions led to an inrush of workers into the national factories and other controlled establishments, with the result that employers and managers were brought face to face with a number of acute problems connected with the health, housing, feeding, and protection of the workers. In order to advise on and supervise these many new problems, a department was set up within the Ministry of Munitions under the directorship of that famous social worker, Mr. B. S. Rowntree. He had with him as collaborator towards the end of the war the Rev. Robert R. Hyde, who from 1916 to 1918 was the Chief Welfare Officer on the boys' side, and is now the Director of the Society. By the end of the war Mr. Hyde had become impressed by the multitudinous ways of doing good that the Welfare office could devise and came to the conclusion that what had been such a boon in war-time should prove equally valuable during peace, if not as a Government department, at least on a voluntary basis. As a result he took steps to form such an organization, using the machinery which had been laid down under State conditions as a guide to the new effort.

It was thus that the Industrial Welfare Society was born, for the purpose of encouraging employers to extend the work which had been so successfully begun in the war period, and to act as a clearing-house of information in connection with the many questions falling within the welfare field—employment, co-operation, education, health, thrift, accident prevention, and leisure interests. Mr. Hyde drew the King's attention to the new Society. Eagerly, and to the delight of the pioneers in it, he accepted the presidency of the new and as yet untried organization. The country has to-day become so thoroughly accustomed to this important phase of his activities that it is sometimes forgotten that in pre-war days there was very little association between members of the Royal Family and industrial life. Public opinion recognized that the members of the Royal Family were in their traditional environment when patronizing the armed forces of the Crown, and since the splendid lead given by Queen Victoria there has never been any lack of recognition of the charitable efforts made by the country. It was not that industry as such was ignored or slighted, it was just that no avenue of approach to the great mass of the workers had been discovered or explored. It remained for the King to find that intimacy of touch between the Royal Family and the ranks of industry which was needed. To-day he is fast becoming a leader in something more than name. Without show, formality, or fuss or bother, he has deliberately and consistently made contact with men of all classes connected with productive enterprise. In shipyards, textile mills, at the coal face, in engineering works, in food-producing concerns, he has had many opportunities of studying at first hand problems and difficulties which have in recent years been prominently before the nation. Already, by his sincerity, his eagerness to understand something of the difficulties of the ordinary employer, his willingness to discuss as man to man the problems of the worker, he has earned a very warm place in the hearts of the industrial population. Industry is to-day seeking some codifying force, some nucleus of inspiration towards a better understanding of each other's view-point, and it may well be that this focal point is being provided by the personality of the King. It is doubtful whether in any other way or in any other field greater contribution could be rendered to the happiness, progress, and harmonious working of all engaged in the vast industrial army of this country.

His method from the first has always been the individual one. To use his own words: "It is the personal touch which counts in creating the mutual sympathy and mutual understanding between the employer and employed which mean so much in the world of industry." The King had long realized the importance of Capital and Labour getting together if Britain's lead in the industrial world was to be maintained. He set out deliberately to achieve an ideal expressed by himself as "cementing that fellowship between individuals in all walks of industry, irrespective of class and occupation, which is the backbone of our Imperial progress." In pursuance of that ideal he strove always to make his visits to factories and shops, his talks with employer and employed, politicians and factory hands alike as informal as possible. He found, he confessed, that the more informal the contact, the greater the amount of information he acquired, and information was what he was after. Many times he has gone round a factory or shop, talked with the workers, and departed again before the hands even knew that it was the King who was showing such a keen and knowledgeable interest in their work.

These visits and those experiences have by now covered a very wide field indeed. Perhaps no one, be he leader of a great trade union or the chairman of a chain of industrial companies, could boast a more extensive knowledge of working conditions all over the world than can the King. He has seen a crude piece of mechanism but little removed from the primitive doing some needful task on a native cotton-field in the Sudan, and he has stood before the " keen, unpassioned beauty of a great machine " in the heart of the most highly industrialized section of the world's surface. From all the wealth of knowledge that lies between those two poles he has garnered a store of detail that as the days go on and the store increases becomes to him more and more valuable. With his early training in electricity and mechanics he grasps the complexities of modern machinery more quickly than the average man, and whenever it is possible he loves to run the thing himself. A score of times he has driven engines. Once in the South Island of New Zealand, in the run from the west coast through the Otira gorge to Christchurch, he was on the footplate nearly the whole afternoon, until he had barely time left in which to change from the suit of greasy overalls to the magnificence of uniform for the ceremonial entry into Christchurch. It was on that occasion that the train touched fifty miles an hour, and fifty miles an hour on a three-foot-six gauge with a track not ballasted with the meticulous care of an English railway is no mean speed. There was a very characteristic incident on that journey, too. A wayside community half-way across the Canterbury plain had gathered by the railway side for a glimpse of the King as the train ran through. They expected, not unnaturally, that they would see a slim, well-tailored, immaculately turned-out young gentleman who would graciously, if formally, acknowledge their loyal greetings. Instead, a beaming coal-streaked face smiled at them delightedly from the engine's cab, a blue-clad arm shot out of the window, and a grimy hand clasping a wad of cotton waste waved a cheery greeting to them. Another time, at the other side of the world—in Glasgow, when he was opening the tramways' department recreation grounds—he drove one of the Corporation trams from the city to the ground. It was rather like the Juggernaut procession, for the streets were crowded with excited Glaswegians, and only an expert touch on the lever saved many of the citizens from the wheels. For those on the driving platform with him it was a hair-raising half-hour, but the King was unperturbed—he knew his machine and how to run it.

Nor is he content with the mere surface survey. If it is a coal mine he wants to see the actual place where the coal is hewed, and that determination led once in South Wales to an amusing contretemps. The party included Mr. Frank Hodge, then First Civil Lord of the Admiralty and secretary of the Miners' Federation of Great Britain. Owing to some misunderstanding about dress, he and his official secretary turned out in full ceremonial attire, top-hat, frock-coat and all. The station-master who welcomed the party naturally thought this resplendent gentleman was the King, who, knowing what was ahead of him, was in tweeds, and bowed deeply before the embarrassed minister, until a prod from another member of the staff swung his obeisance in the right direction. A little later on the miners working at the face had the ineffable pleasure of seeing their general secretary descend the pit in all the glory of a top-hat—and other things, of course. At another mine—the first one he ever went down—the miners, as soon as they knew the King was among them, hurriedly assembled their beloved band to show their appreciation when he again reached the surface. As the time approached the whole district seemed to be gathered at the pit-head, and as soon as the King stepped out of the shaft, blackened from head to foot, the band burst out with the National Anthem, but all their efforts were drowned by the spontaneous outburst from the crowd of " For he's a jolly good fellow." It was on this visit, too, that the King, anxious as ever to " see how the wheels went round," actually handled a pick at the face and hewed out a lump of coal. This lump was afterwards broken up into small pieces as souvenirs, and judging by the numbers of miners' cottages that display one of the small nuggets, the original lump must have been of truly heroic proportions.

The outstanding feature of all these visits has ever been the King's intense interest in the workers' point of view and his ready understanding of their methods of work and general conditions of employment. As a matter of fact, it is safe to say that he is more deeply concerned with these problems than with the latest developments in machinery which will enable the lucky owner to make more money at less expense, or in the most up-to-date application of some new theory in the science of business system. There was one case where he visited a glue factory— not a very savoury place—and the directors proposed that they should shirk the inspection of some of the more unpleasant portions of the establishment. " Why," said the King, " people work there, do they not ? Well, what's good enough for them is good enough for me." And he went through the whole place faithfully and thoroughly. Again he was standing with Mr. Hyde watching a girl conducting some very intricate operation connected with the making of paint-brushes. " What happens when you make a mistake ? " asked Mr. Hyde. The King saw the girl flush and turned to his companion. " Hyde," he reproved, " she never makes a mistake." It is that keenness on the workers' side that has sent him over and over again into their homes ; has seen him in the headquarters of the great trade unions learning so that he might know how the administrative work was carried on and how the officials kept in touch and made themselves acquainted with the needs and aspirations of their members. A treasured memory of those who were with him on a visit to the Natsopa Convalescent Home at Nuneaton, where the old and ailing members of the National Society of Operative Printers and Assistants are cared for, is the picture of him standing bending over the chairs of some of the oldest members of the union, listening almost with tears in his eyes while they told him of the hardships of their early days, their struggles to keep the flag of trade unionism flying against the gales of public execration which blew on it then.

During his Australian and New Zealand tour his official engagements left him little leisure, but he always found time to squeeze out of the precious hours the necessary break to enable him to make some industrial inspection. If he could do it in no other way he made time by getting up before breakfast, as when in a bleak dawn at Greymouth he hurried out—his train left before noon and there were several functions to attend beforehand—to see a Government-controlled mine. He had been told that in that mine he would see how far an advanced democracy had gone in studying the welfare of the workers. Not satisfied with seeing the bath houses, the safety machinery, and the institute where the mental and social needs of the community are ministered to, he walked about the tidy streets of the village, talked with the miners' wives at the doors of their own homes, found out whether and why they liked the system of serving all the creature needs of the workers from one big central store, and satisfied himself that conditions were as good as could be expected, with a benevolent Government holding the balance a little in favour of the workers.

He did the same thing in Wellington. There, a few miles out from the centre of the city at Lower Hutt, the Government had erected a modern village or garden city for the benefit of the workers. The

King, faced with a very full morning of official duties, snatched an hour between two engagements —a municipal welcome and a Government lunch. That was the day when the Police department broke every traffic regulation of the city. As usual, throughout the tour, the King's own car was always preceded by a car carrying three or four members of the police force. It was a good, fast car, and frequently on the North Island tour it had beaten the Royal train between stopping-places. But the King, as do his brothers, holds the opinion that if the thing he is in is movable it ought to move. Moreover, he had only a very little time to spare. So his chauffeur at the Royal bidding " stepped on the gas." An hour or two later a very disconsolate Inspector reported to his Chief Commissioner of Police that they had allowed the King's car to pass them on a level stretch of road a few miles out of the busy city traffic. The Commissioner stormed that they should have ever committed such a grave dereliction of their duty. Their post was two hundred yards ahead of the Royal car, and there they should have remained at all costs. The Inspector protested that they were doing all of fifty miles an hour when the thing happened. " But," he grinned happily, " after all, they weren't long in front, we passed them again a few minutes later." What the actual speed was that the cars were cutting out when the police car did resume its appointed place, history saith not, but there was a mischievous smile on the King's face when the incident of the painful police interview was reported to him a little later in the day. At all events, he had done what he set out to do. He walked through the village, and as usual insisted on seeing things for himself. Several of the cottages had been swept and garnished against his coming, but he disdained this obvious desire to have him see only what had been prepared for him. "We'll go in here," he said, turning up the garden path of a little house whose occupants had been peering stealthily above the window curtains during his progress up the street. There was a scampering of young feet and the door was opened by a very flustered house-wife. "How are you?" said the King pleasantly. "May I come in?" "I'm that excited," was the reply, "I don't know what I'm doing." But the King had her at her ease very quickly, inspecting the arrangements of the pleasantly furnished and scrupulously kept cottage, insisted that the children should be routed out of the various hiding-places where they had taken sanctuary, talked with them about their school and their games, and went away leaving one family swelling with importance and with a topic of conversation that was to last them for many a day.

Such stories so illustrative of his humanity and understanding could be repeated, *mutatis mutandis*, almost *ad infinitum*. Nor does he leave it in any way in doubt that all the incidents of the visits he has made and the contacts he has established have left him with a supreme faith in the capacity of British factories and British industrial concerns generally to handle all requirements. " There is no need," he has told industrial audiences more than once, " to go outside British factories for any goods that may be required for the service of industry itself or for the household use of the public." More than that, the faith in British industry which he so emphatically holds, he holds no less emphatically in regard to the inherent stability of the British worker. He does not—most assuredly he does not —believe that the men he meets as he goes through a machine shop, or the women who flock out from their benches to cheer him and his Queen whenever they appear in their midst, have any revolutionary tendencies whatever—unless it be revolutionary to try and get the best they can out of their life and their work.

During the Australian and New Zealand tour there were many old women—of both sexes—who shook their heads most apprehensively whenever they heard he was going into this or that area, where what have come to be known as " Bolshevist tendencies " were supposed to be rife. Sometimes they even ventured to tell him that the whole country was " honeycombed with Reds." He always had one answer for that. " Show me one," he would say with that disarming smile of his and go on his way rejoicing at every opportunity that was afforded him of getting under the skin of the man in the street. Wherever he went he made it his duty—it was surely his pleasure—to get the other man's point of view, and in getting it, to impress on the man he was talking to that it was over and above everything else his deep abiding interest in his fellow-man that prompted his questions. The mining district on the west coast of New Zealand bears the same reputation among the fearful as does the coal mining area of South Wales here. It is supposed to be more extreme, more revolutionary in tendency than any other district in New Zealand. The member of the district was then the late Mr. H. E. Holland, a man of strong convictions—convictions for which he suffered. The day the King visited the centre of the constituency, Westport, he had to go alone, for the Queen had, only a few hours previously, succumbed to a bad throat attack, and had been left behind at Nelson. But all preparations for the Westport visit had then been made and those preparations included the presentation of a bouquet to the Queen by Miss Holland. Naturally, there was no more disappointed girl on the ground than she was when the Royal party arrived. Her father had, as good fathers will, seen to it that frock and furbelows were all in order and, proud of his daughter, was there too to see the ceremony, though many thought that he would absent himself. The story soon reached the King's ears and he had not been in the town half an hour before Mr. Holland and his daughter were both added to the Royal party and a very happy girl smiled her way to the hotel with a gratified father. The King cancelled the instructions for a private dinner after a hard day's motoring and his two new guests spent the rest of the evening with him. When he went later to the " citizens' ball," where by the way he saw " the Albert " danced in all its ancient magnificence—he took Mr. Holland with him and they sat together on the dais, watching the guests enjoy themselves. For their part the guests were quick to appreciate the courtesy shown their member and leader. They lined up in force as the King left the hall and the chorus, " For he's a jolly good fellow," was as fervent as any he heard throughout the tour. Next morning, the first on the ground to say good-bye was Mr. Holland, and it is safe to say that no more sincere speech of farewell was made than his. The incident ended with two men parting with a profound respect for each other, the King with a store of opinions and facts about the aims and aspirations of the New Zealand Labour Party, its leader with a new conception of Royalty differing materially from the one to which he had in previous years given forcible expression.

In Christchurch, a few days later, a mayor of pronounced Socialist tendencies—a minister of the Gospel and a thoroughly sound administrator— whom the irreverent constantly referred to as " the Bolshie Mayor of Christchurch," went out of his way to give a press interview, devoted to praise of the King whose character, he said, " made a special appeal to the working man." Later still in Sydney it was expected that the Labour Premier, Mr. J. T. Lang, because of his pronounced views might be discourteous to the Royal couple—and was not, except perhaps in the minutiæ of meeting them in a lounge suit instead of the regulation topper and tails. At least, that was all that the censorious could think of in his dispraise after the King and Queen had gone. But the King, knowing that the New South Wales Cabinet of the day had very determined views as to the necessity of restricting migration from the British Isles, had Mr. Lang up to Government House for a long and informative interview and further showed his courtesy by daily inquiries about the health of Mrs. Lang, who was then in a private hospital. The whole attitude of the Labour Party of Australia, so often maligned by interested politicians, was re-expressed and re-emphasized at the great Commonwealth dinner in Melbourne when Mr. Charlton, the leader of the Federal Labour Party, then the official opposition, spoke extempore and in the warmest terms of the visit, and assured the King that whatever the political complexion of the Australian elector and Australian member might be he yielded to none in his loyalty to the Empire and his affection for the Throne. It is safe to say that the words of the veteran leader carried the more weight because by then the character of the King no less than the charm of the Queen had forged a stronger link than ever in the associations of the peoples of Australia with their elder brethren overseas.

There is but one more aspect to stress in this review of the King's devotion to the work of Industrial Welfare. Writing some time ago to the Rev.

Robert R. Hyde, who was then presiding at one of the conferences of the Society, the King crystallized his ideal as follows :

" The fact that members of your conference represent industry in nearly all its forms and undertakings, of almost every size, indicates a growing recognition of a principle for which we have long contended. It is that the only real peace is that which is cultivated in the factory itself.

" Our aim is to create in our workshops such an atmosphere of mutual good-will and fertile partnership that misunderstandings cannot thrive. This is just another instance of that old truth that the quality and happiness of our national life is the quality and happiness of each man and woman. During my visits to the factories and workshops all over the country, I have seen many evidences of the foundations of peace you are quietly and solidly laying, and it must be some satisfaction for your labours to know that it is only upon such firm groundwork that it is possible to erect those signal edifices of co-operation to be seen in the national conferences and conventions we are hearing so much of at the present time.

" It is to be hoped, therefore, that you will be encouraged to continue your very practical efforts to find ever new roads through the complexities of man's daily toil."

That expresses the ambition the King cherishes from day to day. He is modest about it in his

THE KING AND QUEEN TALKING TO AN AUSTRALIAN
VETERAN WHO FORMED ONE OF THE GUARD OF
HONOUR WHEN QUEEN ALEXANDRA LEFT DENMARK
TO MARRY KING EDWARD

THE END OF THE KANGAROO HUNT

public references. Once, for example, he described the Industrial Welfare Society as " merely part of a great attempt to bring about a revival of that spirit of industrial comradeship which has taken hold of masters and men in the past and gradually to restore the old sentiments of friendship which existed many years ago between employer and employed." That may be understating the aims of the Industrial Welfare Society. It is certainly understating the work of the King in that cause. Whatever the aim of the Society may be, the fact is undeniable that the King forms in his own person the pivotal point in its advocacy and its energies.

CHAPTER TEN

THE WORLD TOUR—THE OUTWARD VOYAGE

THE year 1925 may be said, for the purposes of chronology, to mark the commencement of the King's " Imperial " career. Not that he had not before then taken his share, sometimes an onerous one, in the subjects and the functions that fell to the care of Royalty in connection with the reception and recognition of dwellers in the far places of the British Empire. But that interest and association became more consolidated, and accentuated from 1925 onwards. The beginning of that year found him still in East Africa on a trip which, as has been said, was undertaken more in the nature of a holiday but which nevertheless, with the King's unfailing propensity to absorb information from every source possible, left him much the richer in knowledge of a not inconsiderable or unimportant part of the King's dominions. On his return, he found himself plunged into the many duties rendered necessary by the absence of his brother, on his visit to South Africa and the Argentine. These duties included taking over the presidency of the Wembley Empire Exhibition for the second year of its existence. That Exhibition, the second term of which he opened on May 12th,

1925, brought to him a far more extensive acquaintance not only with the products and potentialities of the Empire, but also—and this to him was of much more moment—with the men who came to the Exhibition from various parts of the Empire and told him at the numerous lunches and functions of all kinds something of the lands they lived in. It is safe to say that these meetings fired him with an even greater ambition than before to see for himself, just as soon as it could be managed, something of the far-flung dominions of the Empire.

Therefore when the Federal Government of Australia asked for a King's son to open the Federal Parliament when it moved to the new capital at Canberra, it was the King who was eager to see the new nations of the South, who was selected to represent his father. It was, moreover, peculiarly fitting that he, as Duke of York, should be the one to perform the ceremony. For it was his father who, as Duke of York, had opened the first Commonwealth Parliament in Melbourne on May 9th, 1901. For his son, bearing the same title, to officiate when the Commonwealth came into its own house, appealed to the sense of the fitness of things. The date of the opening was fixed for May 9th, 1927— again the sense of the fitness of things—and the suggestion was made that the intervening months of 1927 should be devoted to a world tour that would take in New Zealand and as many points of the Empire girdle of the world as could be arranged. It need hardly be emphasized with what eagerness the King accepted the suggestion or how keen he was that, having due regard to the time available, he and the Queen should see as much as possible and visit as many places as could be arranged.

With those ends in view a very comprehensive tour was finally mapped out, beginning with Las Palmas in the Canary Islands and ending five months or so later at Gibraltar. Between those two points was listed a most diverse itinerary, with civilisations ranging from the highest the new world of the south had to offer, to the most primitive peoples left in the world to-day, and from cities no less important than those of the British Isles to a string of palm-thatched huts fringing a tropic beach. The battle-cruiser *Renown*, which had already served his elder brother in a similar capacity, was chosen as the " Royal yacht," so to speak, and a staff was organized which would best be calculated to assist the King in what, as everybody knew, would be a most exacting round of public functions. In the event the choice of the members of it proved most happy. As Chief-of-Staff to the King was the Earl of Cavan, Lady Cavan going as Lady-in-Waiting to the Duchess. Lord Cavan had an abounding capacity for detail and his most distinguished military career made him very sure of a welcome wherever he went. The King's personal Secretary, the indefatigable Mr. P. K. Hodgson, had as his opposite number Sir Harry Fagg Batterbee —the title being actually the recognition of his valuable work throughout the tour—whose official

designation was "political secretary" and whose
duties included the advising of the King from the
view-point of the Dominion Office, of which he is
to-day an Assistant Under-Secretary of State. The
Duke's Equerries were Lieutenant-Commander Colin
Buist, R.N., who had been with him to East Africa
and had been for some years on his staff, and Major
(now Lt.-Col.) T. E. G. Nugent, M.C., Comptroller
of Lord Chamberlain's department, while Surgeon-
Commander H. E. Y. White, R.N., was the medical
adviser, as he had been for the Prince of Wales on
previous tours. The Queen had, in addition to
Lady Cavan, the Hon Mrs. Little Gilmour as Lady-
in-Waiting. The whole "team" proved a most
delightful combination not only to those who met
them but to themselves—no small compliment to
their tact and friendliness when it is remembered
that they had to work together for several weeks of
long sea voyages when tempers are sometimes tried
by tropic conditions.

The voyage began on a bleak winter's day—
January 6th, 1927—from Portsmouth. With that
unerring instinct for the sentimental they have
possessed through the centuries, the British people
regarded the departure with more than their usual
interest in the doings of Royalty. The whole
journey, its objects, its circumstances particularly
appealed to their imagination—and in a twofold
manner. First of all there was the King's son
embarking on an Imperial duty as his father had
done before him, to take anew to the people of the

Young Dominions beyond the curve of the world the greetings of their kinsmen in the British Isles, to carry the personal touch of the Throne into the homes of those who not so many years before had stood shoulder to shoulder with them in the trenches, There was that—but there was something else too. Scarcely six months before, the young Princess Elizabeth had come into a world that most eagerly welcomed her. Now, just when her " baby days and baby ways " were becoming most fascinating, her father and mother were leaving her to fulfil an Empire duty. Every woman in the tens of thousands who thronged the approaches to Victoria Station, or stood packed along the Hard and down the beaches to Southsea, or crowded the decks of the shrieking sisterhood of tugs and ferryboats which escorted *Renown* down the Solent, knew just what that meant—and men as well as women reacted to that sentiment. Just as the King himself had been left a small boy in knickerbockers when his father and mother sailed on the Australian tour twenty-six years before, so he and his Queen were going at the same call, leaving their child as King George's young family had been left at the summons of public duty. There was not a man who did not feel the significance of the event ; not a woman who did not sympathize.

Once away from the pomp and circumstance of the departure ceremonial, it was remarkable how quickly affairs on *Renown* slipped back into the accustomed grooves, and with them the King became again the naval officer of a previous decade. The beflagged and " dressed " ship, before the Isle of Wight had faded in the dusk astern, became again the warship, steaming down channel " on her lawful occasions." The sparkling full-dress of officers and the parade uniforms of Marines were doffed, workaday clothes were donned, and what had been a gala ship was once more " in her habit as she lived." And so was the King, who almost before the decks had been cleared of all extraneous matter on the departure had slipped into the well-remembered blue serge and was about the decks, sniffing the well-remembered smells, listening to the well-remembered orders, absorbing delightedly the well-remembered atmosphere of a King's ship abroad on the high seas. For one of the " passengers " that first afternoon at sea carries a charming memory. They were bidden to afternoon tea in the Royal quarters, and as they entered the drawing-room they " surprised " the King and Queen making ready for their guests as would any young host and hostess. The King held poised above his head a large chair, asking plaintively of a gaily laughing Queen where it was to be put. They had evidently done the arranging of the tea-table and chairs themselves, and took full charge of all the tea-pouring and cake-handing when the visitors had settled down at their ease to enjoy their first meeting with the two whose every movement almost they were to follow during the ensuing six months.

As a farewell to winter, the Atlantic sent along a

" regular smeller " of a gale for the second day out,
and *Renown*, fitted with bulges, rolled in the big sea
to a very uncomfortable extent, belying altogether
the assurances of a very famous Admiral on Victoria
platform that whatever the sea, no one on board
would know they were afloat. Most of the landsmen
and landswomen did, though the King and Queen
both braved the weather and were about the ship
most of the day. But very few of their staff were.
The King was very busy for those first few days
at sea. There was a tremendous amount of detail
work in connection with the tour to be sorted out,
and he and Lord Cavan spent hours at the plans
and arrangements for shore functions generally.
Then the ship had to be inspected and every portion
visited both by himself and the Queen, while the
conditions of the crew's quarters and the provision
made for their comfort and well-being were the
King's particular care and interest. The Queen
was no whit behindhand, and insisted likewise on
seeing every part of the big battle-cruiser, from
conning tower to propeller shafting, the engine-room
staff swelling with pride because she was able to
visit every part of their sweltering domain without
the wearing of overalls.

Las Palmas, the first port of call, served the
purpose of a rehearsal, so to speak, for the mechanics
of landing and other ceremonial which had to be
undertaken throughout the tour. Not only the
naval part—that was, as always, well known and
performed—but also the various points of etiquette

and the strict adherence to precedence and so on
which must be observed if all was to go smoothly.
It was a fairly brief visit—barely twenty-four hours
in length—but the little English colony did their
very best to make the stay for the King and Queen
a happy augury for the whole tour, and succeeded
just as well as did the Spanish authorities in their
more formal expressions of welcome and good-will.
The landing was made in the picket boat to the port
of Luz, and a very lively trip it proved, with a big
swell rolling in and a fresh breeze to keep the waves
crisp with scud. Indeed, so nasty was the lop that
the Spanish Governor of the town excused himself
from going on board *Renown*, and paid his respects
at the landing-stage instead. From there the Royal
party drove to various functions along dreadful
roads through dingy streets. There they disputed
the right-of-way with a rickety tram-car, strings of
laden mules or milch goats. The island presents
the anomaly that while the motor-cars it accom-
modates are among the most luxurious and as well
kept as any in the world, there are no railways, the
only approach to anything of the sort being the afore-
said tram-line from the port to Las Palmas itself.
The explanation is that before the community was
rich enough to afford the luxury of railway travel,
the motor-car and motor lorry had been so far
developed that they took the place of the locomotive
and the freight-car, even although to-day the
motors still have as competitors for freight the mule
and the bullock of primitive peoples. Now, of

course, Las Palmas is a prosperous community, thanks to the banana and other semi-tropical fruits, and the English residents on the island are making it a very pleasurable living-place. The King was able to see there how a Spanish settlement, perhaps belonging more to past centuries than the present, has had grafted on to it a " garden city " and a " seaside resort " more in accordance with the English idea of how life should be lived. The English families who follow their business there have seen no reason why they should not be as well furnished with the amenities of social life as their kinsmen in the outer suburbs of London. So the English club flourishes and the English villa stands side by side with the high blank walls and heavy gateways of the typical Spanish town house of a hundred years or more ago. They have " colonized " two localities all to themselves, a pleasant little seaside bungalow town with excellent bathing almost from one's own verandah and a more elaborate " garden city " which has sprung up about midway between the port and the town proper. Las Palmas is not so popular a tourist place as Madeira, though there is considerable traffic, and therefore the Duke saw more clearly how the English who stay there from year's end to year's end do manage to make themselves comfortable in foreign surroundings.

The voyage across the Atlantic from the Canaries to the West Indies served to settle the ship's company into the routine which they were to follow for so many weeks of tropical and subtropical sailing. The King himself parcelled out his day in most methodical fashion. The mornings were spent with Lord Cavan and the other members of the staff discussing multitudinous points of detail. He was in constant wireless touch not only with London but also with New Zealand and Australia, and kept himself very thoroughly abreast of all the arrangements and alterations that were for ever being made. Then there were speeches to be written and revised, questions of precedence and etiquette to be settled, problems of how to fit in all the many functions suggested to him. He never spared himself in these tasks. After lunch, which was taken at the usual Navy hour, with the usual Navy " stretch off the land " to follow, there came the hours of exercise. In vest and shorts the King applied himself strenuously to the business of keeping himself fit. Most often he chose for his partners or competitors the officers of the ship ; sometimes it was a member of his staff, and at others a vigorous game of deck tennis saw him opposed to the Queen with a Lady-in-Waiting for his partner and an equerry for hers. Invariably after the exercise there was a visit to the ward-room, where in the most unconventional manner, and in the most unconventional garb, the King chatted with the men who happened to be present and joined cheerily in all the chaff and ragging that went on. After dinner, at which there were always three or four officers of gun-room or ward-room present as guests, in addition to the personal staff, the King and Queen usually came down to the quarter-deck where more often than not the gramophone provided music for a merry little impromptu dance in which the Queen and her Ladies-in-Waiting were naturally greatly sought after as partners. This daily programme was varied occasionally by the Royal party being entertained in turn by either the gun-room or the ward-room, or by concerts and cinema shows on the quarter-deck, to the former of which many lower-deck stars contributed with much success.

In Jamaica, which was reached on the 20th January, there was one touch of romance that is worth recording among all the official and semi-official functions, the motor-car rides and dancing of a modern and very pleasure-loving community. One morning early the King slipped away from the side of *Renown*, one of the finest examples of the most modern fighting machine afloat, and crossed the Kingston roads to Port Royal, that place of famous and infamous memory where the "careless captains" roistered and revelled, where men slaked their passions after months of piracy and buccaneering among the islands of the Spanish main, and where licence gave place at last to law and the British Navy took charge and made it into a Naval station. It was there in the years before his greatness that Nelson was posted, and there the King saw Fort Charles, where Nelson was wont to pace the ramparts as he would a quarter-deck, telescope under arm and weather eye lifting seaward for the French fleet. The whole of Port Royal, indeed, bedraggled and faded as it now is, is redolent of memories of the Navy, for its churches and barracks are full of memorials, among them tributes to many midshipmen of twelve and thirteen years old who had died on the station from the dreaded yellow fever or at sea as a result of " falls from aloft." The King spent much time there, while across the waters of of the harbour the new navy, in the shapes of the two escorting cruisers of the West Indian station, the *Calcutta* and *Colombo*, waited at attention for his inspection. The two navies joined hands as it were when he came alongside the former, for he was piped overside by the bosun's mates as he would have been at any time since the British Navy took the sea. Indeed, there are few if any places in the world where the old and the new are so linked as they are in Jamaica. It is in Spanish Town that Rodney's tomb lies, and memorials to English sailors there date back to the seventeenth century, and many were the ships of Elizabethan captains from Drake downwards which lay in its harbours or careened on its beaches. It was here and hereabouts that the sea story of Britain was begun, " the nursery of the British Navy " as Sir Frederick Treves has termed it.

Contrasts of another sort awaited the King four days' sail from Jamaica when *Renown* reached Colon and the Caribbean entrance to the Panama Canal, that mighty monument to the thoroughness and efficiency of the United States. As the big ship passed up the outer reaches of the canal to the Gatun dam she travelled virtually the channel of the Chagres river. It was up that river two and a half centuries before that Morgan and his twelve hundred scoundrels crept in canoes to the sack of old Panama on the other side of the Isthmus. The ruins of that city—founded in 1518—lie only a few miles away from Balboa, where the Americans have erected one of the most modern of residential quarters for the canal employees, while between the two extremes, as it were, lies " new " Panama, new only by comparison for it was founded in 1673 after the destruction of old Panama. Much of it still bears the imprint of the seventeenth century in its massive churches, built to the greater glory of God it is true, but with thick walls to defy the attacks of pirates and raiders, in its narrow ill-kept streets and typical Spanish architecture. And alongside these evidences of the past are the very modernly designed buildings which the Americans have added to the city or which are reminders of the Panama Exposition of 1916. The Royal visit was brief, but it had moments of interest, as when the King paid his official visits to the President of the Panama Republic and to the American Governor. The utmost punctilio, intensely Spanish in character, was observed on this occasion. *Renown* was, of course, in the American zone as she lay at the Balboa wharf, so that a troop of American cavalry escorted the Duke across the zone to the point where Panama city began. There a squadron of Panamanian cavalry took over the task, and with much jingling of accoutrements and flashing of sabres formed a bodyguard to the door of the presidential palace. The call over, the procedure was reversed and the American troops " took over " from the Panamanians at the borderline and brought the King back to the Administration buildings where the Governor awaited him.

With Panama astern the long trek to Australia was begun, enlivened by two outstanding incidents, one the ceremony of crossing the line and the other the visit to the remote and lovely Marquesas Islands. For the former, the ship's company really laid themselves out for a most elaborate function, in which the King and the Royal party took their full part. The day began the night before if the Irishism be permitted, with the hailing of the warship by Neptune, who came aboard in full majesty next morning. The King was the first to be barbered and dipped. He entered thoroughly into the spirit of fun that was abroad that day, early earning a joyous tribute from the ratings when he gave instructions to " splice the main brace." Gaiety continued through the day, for in the evening the ward-room had designed a most elaborate restaurant and cabaret show on the quarter-deck, to which the King and Queen came in a taxi manufactured from two of Lord Cavan's invalid-chairs with which he used to get about when the injury to his leg was troubling him. Each member of the Royal party was the guest of three ward-room members and the fun was glorious even although they would insist on

dancing Sir Roger—on the Equator too—until the
band gave up in exhaustion.

Dancing of a very different sort awaited the King
and Queen at the little port of Tai-o-hae of Nukohiva,
one of the Marquesas Islands where *Renown* went to
oil. There still dwells a remnant of the mighty tribes
which thronged the islands in the days when Whyte
Melville wrote *Typee*, and from their ranks the
French Resident had drawn a few " troupes " of
men and women who still remembered or who had
learnt from their elders the old native dances.
The entertainment was given in front of the
Resident's house at night, in the flare of kerosene
torches, while the thousand lights of the warship
in the bay below laid a pathway of radiance across
the calm waters. As is the case with so many dances
of the primitive type, the movements were of the
body as much as of the feet. The women were for
the most part immobile from the waist up, trusting
to their hips and legs for movement, with an occasional wave of the hand to give some point to the
softly crooned accompanying song. The men were
much freer in their movements, throwing their arms
and legs about in vigorous action. The " troupes,"
which consisted of five men and five women, came
from different villages, and most of them had special
dance forms of their own. One of the most popular,
which was danced by the men alone, was supposed
to represent a wild pig in search of a wife. All the
time it was being danced the men gave vent to a
continuous grunting sound which seemed to come

Speaight

THE KING IN THE UNIFORM HE WORE AT CANBERRA

AT A BOY SCOUTS' REVIEW IN ADELAIDE WITH
GENERAL "TOM" BRIDGES

right from their diaphragm, most realistically imitative of the wild boar. The music was supplied by the voices of the dancers singing in four-part melody and by a collection of drums ranging from one that had evidently begun its life in a French infantry band to a converted petroleum tin which its owner, presumably from one of the more penurious islands, manipulated with surprising effectiveness. The subject-matter of the dances was not explained in detail, but it plainly had to do with the preoccupations of a savage race—with hunting, with the preparation of food, and particularly with love-making. Indeed, in one the chase of the fair but frail one was most vividly pictured, a double line of men alternately capturing and losing their Polynesian Helens. With it all though, the decorous damsels with the downcast eyes who shyly went through all the motions and the men who very obviously were restraining their full-blooded ideas of what a dance should be, must have been but a pale adumbration of what would have been seen a half-century or more before, when the Marquesians were reputed to be the handsomest and most immoral of all the Polynesians and indulged in terrific orgies until the French missionaries led them into the gentler arts of Christianity. There was nevertheless one moment when the dance in progress did threaten to lapse into its earlier " freedom " had not a hurried and very flustered master of ceremonies plunged into the ranks and peremptorily stopped it. One other incident of the two days' stay in the Marquesas

must linger in the King's memory. He was taken
down the coast to a little village tucked away in the
folds of one of the gigantic volcanic valleys that
everywhere radiate out from the central basaltic
massif. There the villagers, not, it is to be feared,
without a certain pagan pride, haled forth to meet
the Royal party an old veteran. He, they explained,
was a genuine cannibal who could tell of huge feasts
of human flesh which were held in the Meae or
sacred enclosure still to be seen in the centre of the
huts.

Polynesian ceremonial of quite another kind
awaited the King and Queen at Fiji, the last place
visited before reaching New Zealand. The Fijian,
though once one of the most savage and warlike of
the tribes inhabiting the Pacific Islands, was always
chivalrous in his devotion to his chief but ruthlessly
ferocious to his enemies. Now only the chivalry
remains, and of that exquisite politeness and
scrupulous observance of ritual the King had early
demonstration when he attended a native gathering
on the afternoon of arrival. There was no dancing,
an outbreak of measles in the other islands having
prevented the dancers from coming to Suva, but
two most interesting examples of native ceremonial
had been arranged. The first was the presentation
to the King of the Tambua, the whale's tooth which
was symbolic of the act of fealty and homage to the
chief. In the old days the people of his villages
swam out to his canoe as he voyaged along the coast,
but the King had to be content with it being borne

to him by one of the paramount chiefs across the green lawn of the recreation ground. This chief was a magnificent specimen of a man, and in his native dress of tappa cloth, with heavy necklaces of sharks' teeth, his hair brushed out in an aureole round his heavily painted face, he epitomized the old-time dignity and might of the Fijian warrior caste. The women then went through, for the benefit of the Queen, the ceremony of Qalowaqa, a kindred act of homage only paid to chieftainesses of the highest rank. Two long lines of native women in skirts of many-folded tappa cloth and garlanded with flowers drew across the lawn a model of a double canoe such as the Fijians used to build. Its bows were splashed with water as it drew near the Royal dais to signify its passage through the surf, and chanting, always slowly, the women withdrew again as the Queen was also presented with the whale's tooth symbol. The whole ritual was brought to an end with the " drinking in " of the paramount chief. The *yaqona* or *kava*, to give it its more usual name, had to be prepared with all due and proper rites, though fortunately for the King and his staff the old method of chewing it into a thick viscid mass and then diluting it with water has been abandoned in favour of reducing it to a powder first, and then mixing it. Though, truth to say, there are, so it is said, still stalwarts of the old school who maintain that the only way to prepare it is the old-fashioned way. But the rites of preparation remain and very solemnly they were performed. The King was the first to drink from the bowl presented to him by another of the chiefs, and after a tentative sip he drained it, as he was expected to do, spinning the bowl out across the turf afterwards to show that it was empty. Some of the King's staff had to follow suit, and not always did they appear to enjoy the acrid taste of the liquid, to judge by the expressions on their faces. It is rather worth noting that the King was the third of his house for the Fijians to " drink in." His Majesty King George V was the first when a midshipman on the *Bacchante*, and the Duke of Windsor also tasted *kava* when he visited Suva in 1920.

But perhaps the most picturesque of all the native incidents which were the King's portion in Suva, was one quite unconnected with ceremonial. When the Royal party emerged from Government House after the formal dinner to go on to the ball in their honour at the Grand Pacific Hotel they found waiting for them an escort of stalwart Fijians naked to the waist, their skins glistening in the flame of high torches. These barbaric looking men formed up round the motor-car and ran alongside of it all the way to the hotel, their voices raised in a booming war song. When the King and Queen arrived they found waiting for them again a bodyguard of spear-men, who stood all through the reception, one at each corner of the dais, immobile and at attention, the four being relieved at frequent intervals. When the dance was over the Royal couple were again escorted to the landing place by their torch-

men, and as their boat shoved off for *Renown*,
a typical native chant of farewell followed them
across the smooth waters of Suva harbour. It is
characteristic of the King that although anyone
else might have been excused for thinking that the
official programme was strenuous enough, he seized
the opportunity of a " couple of hours off " early in
the morning of the second day, to slip away quietly
with a single Fijian official to make a tour of the
harbour and the near-by villages so that he might
take with him some impressions other than those
which the arranged schedule had provided.

CHAPTER ELEVEN

THE WORLD TOUR—NEW ZEALAND

BEFORE they had even set foot on the shores of New Zealand, which they reached on February 22nd, the King and Queen were " mobbed " by the enthusiastic people of Auckland. *Renown* steamed up the wide waters of Hauraki Gulf to her anchorage in Waitemata, as the Auckland harbour is called, under a grey sky and surrounded by all manner of craft from the flag-bedecked ferry steamer crowded with excursionists to the cheeky little outboard motor which made more noise than the battle-cruiser did. Rain broke as the anchor dropped and drenched the crews and passengers of the scores of boats which clustered round *Renown*. The programme required the King and Queen to leave for the shore in the launch, and tradition requires that when Royalty leaves a ship the Royal Standard is lowered from the foremast to be hoisted again on the launch. Further, when the Standard is lowered, a salute is fired and all activity ceases while the " Still " brings everybody to a halt. Even the launch had to stop its engines, and that was the signal for the occupants of the harbour craft. Untroubled by any Navy tradition or any preoccupation as to Navy ceremonial, the one idea they had was to get as close as possible to the King and Queen and secure a treasured glimpse of the Royal couple just as soon and for as long as they could. So, to the horror of the sticklers for Naval etiquette, the launch became the centre of a milling mass of all sorts and conditions of boats, even to a racing four-oar which added itself to the confusion at imminent peril of damage to its frail hull. As long as the salute took to fire so long was the launch surrounded, so long were the smiling King and Queen the focus of all eyes. Then the engines turned again and the launch drew away shoreward, still accompanied by its self-appointed escort.

Indeed, the chief impression of Auckland borne away by the King and Queen could well be that it was there that they were most often " mobbed." For the enthusiastic crowds which thronged the streets for the procession on arrival broke down all barriers and overwhelmed the burly constables on duty— though these police had been chosen for their physique from all over the Dominion. Barriers were swept away and the Royal car was again the rallying-point of a surging mass, so that progress became almost impossible and then only at a snail's pace, until the police by strenuous endeavour gained control once more. Again, in the afternoon, when the King and Queen were taken on a sight-seeing tour of the city and suburbs, they left their car to walk through the beautiful Ellerslie gardens. Once again the police could not keep the enthusiasts within bounds, and for many minutes all that could be seen in the centre of the maelstrom was an occasional glimpse of the Queen's hat or the King's head. They took the incident as all in the day's work, feeling that the thorough good-humour of the crowd and their manifest delight in being so close to their visitors amply repaid them for any inconvenience. The incident of the children at the big demonstration in the Domain has already been described, while the final scene of all, when the Royal party left the municipal reception for *Renown* at a time nearing midnight, kept up the reputation the Auckland people had earned of being irresistible whenever they made up their minds that they wanted to see the King and Queen—at any rate the police who struggled vainly to stem the tide must have thought so.

A very exacting programme—too exacting, as events turned out, for the Queen—had been prepared for the New Zealand tour, and the authorities had thoughtfully provided a break for sport and relaxation before it was embarked upon. After the Auckland visit, therefore, *Renown* went north to the Bay of Islands, where there is to be found some of the best game fishing in the world. The fascination of the contemplative man's recreation can nowhere be more thoroughly exploited than in the Bay of Islands and the coastal waters immediately outside. There you may find yourself fast in a swordfish or a black marlin or a mako shark which will give you a day-long fight, and turn the scales when you have triumphantly brought him to shore at Russell at anything up to 800 pounds. Indeed, it is on record that one black marlin caught by Captain Mitchell, an English enthusiast, was too big for any of the weighing appliances at Russell and had to be cut in half before its weight could be measured. Even then the two halves weighed 976 lb., so that, making allowances for wastage in the cutting-up process, it is reasonable to assume that had it been put intact on the scales it would have registered the 1000 lb. It is always the biggest fish that gets away, of course, but Zane Grey, the American novelist, who has fished there for years from a most luxurious camp, and Captain Mitchell claim that once they found themselves fast to a fish that must have been all of 1200 lb. These fish, particularly the swordfish and the black marlin, fight with almost incredible ferocity. A black marlin will hurl itself out of the water and batter itself to death on the sheer-faced cliffs of the small islands in the bay. The first instinct of the swordfish when struck is to leap yards clear of the water in an endeavour to throw the hook, and both of them will tow the heavy motor-boats from which the fishing is done for hours before they can be brought to the gaff. Apart altogether from the thrill and excitement of this kind of fishing, the angler can enjoy almost any other variety. The waters teem with fish. There are surface fish such as the mackerel—like khaiwhai, which will take any kind of bait that may be trolled

for them and make, themselves, excellent lure for
the swordfish. There are fast-swimming fish such
as the bonito and the kingfish which prey on the
khaiwhai, while on the " floor " of the harbour
are innumerable schnapper, grouper, harpaka and
other extremely edible fish running up to twenty
and thirty pounds weight, avid for the hook and
affording the fisherman uninterrupted sport. An
hour's fishing will yield a bag of anything up to a
hundredweight and sometimes more, and fish can
apparently be taken at any time or at any state of
the tide. Both the King and the Queen were
out on both days which were spent there, and though
the real big fish eluded the King—the Queen
was content with schnapper fishing—he took a shark
of about two hundred pounds weight.

New Zealand is, indeed, singularly fortunate in
the attractions it possesses as a holiday and sight-
seeing resort. From the excitements of deep sea
fishing, the King and Queen went to the extraordinary thermal region of Rotorua, that marvellous
area of some three hundred square miles where the
volcanic forces are so near the surface that steam
spurts at the walker from the road-side, where hot
springs bubble from the ground at your feet and
run off down the gutters of the town itself ; where
gargantuan porridge pots churn horridly and spit
gobs of mud at unwary spectators, and where
geysers in " Prince of Wales' feathers " soar
hundreds of feet into the air. Here is a guide book
description of another centre of thermal activity

not very far away at Wairekei, where the King and the Queen were also taken, that gives a picture not at all exaggerated of the infernal activities of the region :

" The earth rumbles and shakes from the action of the titanic forces beneath. Vast clouds of steam float away from the valley. The visitors are guided for two hours or more among geysers that play with clock-like regularity at brief intervals, some sinister and threatening, others beautiful and fairylike. Some are at the bottom of the valley and others among the most beautiful verdure of the hill-side. Mud springs—some black and forbidding, others quaint, beautifully tinted and dainty in their ever-changing formations, are everywhere. Weird hob-goblin noises and hisses and titanic throbs continue perpetually. For three hours the visitor sees new and wonderful sights. At the foot of the valley all the accumulations of heated water rush in a large stream into a lake basin—some million gallons a day—from which it disappears into some hidden mysterious depths, the only evidence of its escape being a fearsome metallic sound as of giant blows on a mammoth anvil which comes from somewhere below. There, too, is the most remarkable blow-hole in the world—the safety valve so to speak of the district."

The visit to Rotorua had a double purpose—sightseeing for one and for the other an opportunity of seeing the Maori in their own home surroundings, for the district is the centre of the most prolific of the Maori legends and history. The Government, therefore, wisely encourage them to regard the region as their own special preserve, so to speak, and there, whenever there is a Royal visit, the people of " the other race " flock to do them honour. The Maori is of all the native Pacific races the most interesting and in many respects the most civilized. Their origin is still a matter of debate, but they came first to New Zealand five hundred years ago, after voyaging across the ocean wastes in their large double canoes. When Captain Cook discovered New Zealand they were a savage, ruthless, cruel nation, waging continual tribal wars and universally addicted to cannibalism. British rule and British missionary effort have changed all that and to-day the Maori is one of the most law-abiding and eagerly receptive members of the community. He suffers no inferiority complex, is as proud of his Maori blood as any noble of the ancient regime, and regards himself as the equal in all things of his British neighbour. But they still preserve, still love many of their native customs, and among these relics of a bygone time their passion for music and dancing finds full expression in their *hakas* and *poi* dances, of which the King and Queen were to see many examples, and in one day at Rotorua were to witness a truly magnificent display—the finest, many said, of them all.

The *haka* is the warrior dance, of which there are several variants. The keynote of most of them is the desire to frighten the enemy, and therefore the dancers indulge in the most terrifying gesticulations and grimaces they can invent. Even under the refining influences of civilization the *haka* still exercises a strange power over the Maori, however educated he may be. At one of the displays the organizer was Sir Apirana Ngata, a member for the Eastern Maoris and a very polished speaker in the House of Representatives. Yet before the end of the performance he was among the dancers giving full rein to the old spell. The *poi* dance is the dance of the women. The *poi* itself is a small ball about the size of a fives ball, made of flax and hanging to a long string. These *pois* the girls swing rhythmically to and fro in all manner of intricate twirlings, crooning at the same time very tuneful melodies, while their *piupius* or skirts of flax sway gracefully from their hips. The demonstration, which began with the presentation to the King and Queen of many symbolic articles of Maori craftsmanship, including a wonderful native mat of feathers which the King wore throughout, was a truly magnificent spectacle in the strong sunlight and brisk breeze. The men's naked bodies glistened with perspiration as they thundered through their terrifying war dances, their limbs working spasmodically, their faces contorted, their lips slavering, their bodies writhing, as they worked up the frenzy of all the old tribal passions of hate and fury and revenge. In and out of their ranks, hundreds of Maori girls swayed in long lines with cadenced tread, their bodies bending with sinuous grace, their arms gracefully swinging their *pois*, the flicker of which had at times almost an hypnotic effect. The men wore their flax mats or cloaks of *kiwi* feathers, though sometimes the pagan effect was spoiled by the revelation of a very modernly coloured suit of silk pyamas underneath the savage clothes or by a pair of brogues stamping out the time alongside the naked feet of greater sticklers for the rigour of the game. The girls either also wore mats with their flax skirts, or else just ordinary brightly coloured blouses or jumpers. The young girls were very graceful, very stately in their carriage, but the Maori, like most native races, run to plumpness in maturity, and there were some excellent specimens of solidity among the performers of both sexes.

From Rotorua the King and Queen went to a most charming " rest camp " the Government had had built for them close to the shores of Lake Taupo. The site was withdrawn far from all chance of interference and the tents were set in a woody glade by the musical waters of the Tongariro river. There they were left for two days in almost complete privacy, only Lord Cavan and Lieutenant-Commander Buist for the King, and Lady Cavan for the Queen, remaining with them. Fishing for trout was the main object of the camp, but the fish were not very kind in the stream, though in the Lake parties were taking fine creels of seven to ten-pounders—and hoping for one of the monsters of twenty-five pounds or so which are said to lurk far out in the Lake. But it was a very peaceful time, fit preparation for the strenuous days ahead. New Zealand is a country of small communities, all of whom thought that they should be honoured by a visit from the King's son and all of them seeing no reason at all why any other town or village should have that pleasure instead of them. It must have been a very unenviable task for the Government to decide which towns should be left out, and doubtless the local member had a very unrestful time as well. Certainly, the Government did its best. From first to last in the three weeks of travelling through the country, the King heard fifty-three mayors or other local magnates of provincial towns or districts read fifty-three warmly loyal addresses. The programme of these official receptions hardly ever varied in its essential features. The King and Queen stepped from their train or motor on to some improvised dais. They were welcomed to the particular township by the " local body representatives " as the official programme somewhat ambiguously referred to them. Then the wives were presented, while veterans of many wars and the ex-Service men came in for a share of attention. The Girl Guides and Boy Scouts were next in order of precedence and after that the school children had their turn. Each of them had a flag and a voice and they used both to the maximum of advantage. If there was time there was a short trip to some point of local interest and then the journey was resumed. The period spent in any one town varied from an overnight rest to two minutes, the latter being Feilding's proud record.

But though officially the programme was the same, all sorts of intrusive happenings, most of them unrehearsed, enlivened the trip and added the zest of humour to what otherwise might have been somewhat dull and uninteresting. Many are the stories that could be told illustrative at one and the same time of the King's never-waning desire to learn things for himself and of his intense anxiety to see that everybody possible should meet him and the Queen under the most favourable circumstances. At Palmerston North, for instance, he saw to it that a New Zealand farmer who had once been a shepherd at Sandringham should be given an opportunity of coming in from his holding some miles away with his family and talk with the King and Queen. It was at Palmerston North, too, that lacking other opportunities, he got up well before breakfast and motored out to a butter factory—a visit he did not forget either, for he referred to it two years later, in a speech he made in London. At Napier, when they had both been in the train all day on a long and tiring journey through the Manawatu gorge and the hot plains of the Hawke's Bay district, the people who had been cheering them, it seemed continuously, since they arrived, assembled outside their hotel after dark and clamoured in chorus, " We want the Duke, we want the Duchess." Then, though an easeful time in comfortable chairs would have better suited their moods, both of them went out on to the balcony

TAKING THE TRAIN ACROSS THE NEW
ZEALAND ALPS

Central News

HIS FAVOURITE SPORT

more than once, and bowed and smiled to the tumultuous throng. At Masterton on the way back to Wellington the Queen met and chatted for some time with Sergeant Bennett of the Black Watch, who had been with her brother, Captain Bowes-Lyon, when he was killed at Loos. Then again at Wellington, though he had had a gruelling day with the official functions which were allotted to the Capital, the King squeezed in visits to several factories between a lunch and a garden party, just as in the morning of the same day he had rushed out in the motor to the Workers' Homes on the Lower Hutt.

With the commencement of the tour of the South Island came the one great disappointment of the visit to New Zealand, for at the end of the first day the Queen had most reluctantly to give in to an attack of tonsilitis and return to Wellington in *Renown*. It had been an exacting day with both train and motor journeys, the latter over roads not altogether smooth as macadam and very dusty. The pace set was necessarily rather fast and the combined exertion of sitting erect all day and smiling —as only the Queen can smile—at all the spectators, or meeting the local dignitaries in the half-dozen towns they passed through, proved too much for her. So at the end of the day in Nelson she went straight to her room, hoping that a rest would straighten things out. It did not. Tonsilitis and a high temperature declared themselves, and at midnight the decision was made. It was a blow not only to the expectant inhabitants of the South

Island who had been looking forward to the joint visit with such eagerness, but also to the King who had been so unflaggingly helped and abetted by his wife in all he had done to make the tour a success. He had to content himself with daily talks with her on telephone lines sometimes fixed up by the Government operators across all sorts of improvised circuits. From the day they said good-bye and she returned to Wellington, until they were re-united on *Renown* at the end of the tour, the King hardly missed one night. He talked long and sympathetically to her, telling her all the incidents of the day and discussing with her all manner of questions and problems for future solution.

Had it not been for the deep disappointment the departure of the Queen brought to the King, the tour of the South Island would have proved far more enjoyable than the journeys through the North Island. For one thing, the whole machinery had shaken down, so to speak, and the recurrent receptions became more of a matter of routine of which everybody " knew the drill," and the many changes of costumes and changes of outlook alike were undertaken with far less sense of stress. Then there were the most extraordinary manifestations of mass loyalty at Christchurch—especially at Christchurch—at Dunedin, and indeed everywhere the King went. At Christchurch, which prides itself on being the most English of New Zealand cities, the people really laid themselves out to show how much they appreciated the King's visit. Of all the many instances of this, one must suffice. The night he spent with the " Diggers " has already been referred to. On another evening when he was to be present at a citizens' ball, his car had to move at the slowest of speeds through a densely packed mass of cheering people who for a mile from his hotel ignored all traffic rules and all attempts of the police to clear a passage while they surged up to and almost over the car in their exuberant pleasure at having the King so near to them. Again at Dunedin, which in contradistinction to Christchurch prides itself on being Scotch, there had been a very natural disappointment when they heard that the Queen was not to be with the King. There was in consequence a lull in the sale of tickets for the citizens' ball. But the evening of his arrival, when, in spite of the keen wind of early autumn, the King insisted on his car being changed from the closed limousine which had been provided for him into an open car, so that everybody might see him, clinched the people's opinion of him. Next morning the sale of tickets recommenced in an almost feverish rush, and all through the visit his popularity grew by what it fed on so that university students towed his car for furlongs along the streets and the populace stood for hours waiting for a glimpse of him along any of the routes he was announced to take.

Moreover, there were to lighten the more serious side many incidents that brought the chuckle of appreciation to the lips. For instance, there was the reception at a small mining town where they

had dragged the piano into the middle of the main
—and only—street and the children, while they
sang " God Save the King," vigorously waved the
" Stars and Stripes "—it is not known whether
under a mistaken impression that it was the National
Flag or simply because the larger towns had by
that time bought up the whole available stock of
Union Jacks. There was the lone prospector, sole
resident of what had once been a prosperous mining
centre before the reef worked out, who saw no
reason why he should not present an address of
welcome, and therefore stood in the middle of
the road wildly waving a sheaf of papers as the
King's car sped by. At Murchison the local body
of the small settlement had arranged the reception
in an open space which was intended one day perhaps
to be the town square. There they had erected a
dais, but as the road was dusty they had thoughtfully
borrowed a roll of Chinese matting from the local
Selfridge's and laid it down from the dais to the
steps of the hotel where the King was to lunch.
It was obvious from the first that they regarded the
matting as sacred only to the Royal foot. They had
stationed three or four officials at intervals along its
length and whenever the foot of a wandering press-
man or a member of the staff happened to tread on it
he was startled by a hoarsely whispered admonition
to " Git orf the carpet." When the proceedings
were over and the King walked to the hotel, two
men followed on their hands and knees behind him
carefully rolling the carpet up as he went, so that

no other impious foot should mar its pristine purity. At another mining town where there was a banquet, one of the elder brethren who had helped to found the district dined not wisely but too well, and became obsessed with the idea that he must clap the King on the shoulder. He nearly accomplished his scheme at the first time of asking, and thereafter, spurred by that early success, it took all the ingenuity of the staff, backed by most of the other diners, to ward off the successive attempts he made after every succeeding addition to his " alcoholic content." It must be confessed, however, that the King in high good-humour made the task all the more difficult by deliberately courting the accolade.

Further to the south, again at a mining town, he was asked solemnly by the mayor to " treasure this unique gift." The said " unique gift " was an address of welcome of which there were already nearly half a hundred specimens in the Royal baggage. At Ashburton, which lies in the centre of the rich pastoral country of the South Island where all the Canterbury lamb comes from, the decorations of the dais thoughtfully took in the emblems of the district's prosperity, and the King sat between two pillars of painted wood forming a hollow square in which swung two magnificent carcasses of lamb. The day was distinctly warm, and the carcasses, though straight from the refrigerating chamber, soon began to sizzle in the heat and to revolve on their own axis as though they were turning on a spit in front of a roaring fire. The

King declared afterwards that he felt sure that he was to be served with lamb chops for lunch and was very disappointed when he learnt the real reason for the illusion. His last day in the Dominion was a stormy one, and at Invercargill the local children had subscribed their pennies for a gift to the little Princess Elizabeth. They must have ransacked the whole island for the largest *kewpie* possible, which was duly presented to the King, who regarded it with embarrassment for a moment, then, with a quickness of decision that did him credit, passed the burden over to his equerry and turned his attention to something less in the nursery line. A few hours after that episode he boarded *Renown* again, and the last act in the Dominion was typical of the spirit of the British Navy. There was a howling gale of wind and rain, and so bad were conditions that the idea of taking him out on the small cruiser *Diomed* into the roadstead where *Renown* lay had to be abandoned. Instead, the services of a tug, which proudly flew the Royal Standard, had to be requisitioned, and on her reeling decks the King and his staff made their way to the battle-cruiser just dimly discernible in the mist. The tug came up to leeward, but she was so lively that there was no chance of running the brows out and the passengers had to make their way on board as best they could across the bulwarks of the tug on to the quarter-deck whenever the two levels coincided, which was not often. The King " made an excellent landing," so to speak, nimbly crossing from the bridge of the tug to the guard-rail of *Renown*, where two stalwart ratings caught him in their arms and helped him over the rail, while the Queen watched anxiously from an upper scuttle. The arrival on the quarter-deck could not by any stretch of imagination be called dignified. Yet for all that he was piped overside in traditional fashion by the bosun's mates. He was a King's son returning to the deck of his own ship and due honour must be done him. In any case, many another Admiral had doubtless come aboard in past centuries in far more undignified circumstances. So ended the four weeks' tour of one of the newest of the new Commonwealths of Nations. As the King said in his farewell message, it had been one of the happiest months of his life.

CHAPTER TWELVE

THE WORLD TOUR—AUSTRALIA

WITH the approach to Australia a more serious air began to distinguish the King and his staff. Hitherto, despite the periods of formality here and there, the holiday spirit would not be suppressed. Travel certainly had been prolonged, but the extended ocean voyages and the thoughtful provision by the New Zealand Government of a few days now and again for " rest and refreshment " had kept the feeling of a tourist trip well to the fore. But Australia was quite in a different category. The King had come fifteen thousand miles to act as his father's representative at functions the most solemn and epoch-making in the Commonwealth's history. He was meeting for the first time in their own land a people who had won to nationhood through a century and a half of strong endeavour, a people who began their Federal life while men from their forces were yet fighting in South Africa and who had set the seal on that nationhood with four years of grim warfare in Gallipoli, in France, in Palestine, and in Mesopotamia—wherever the British forces were there were also some units, even some individuals, who owned Australia as their birthplace. Now, having turned once more to the arts of peace, they had determined that their federal parliament should have a home of its own. True that determination preceded the World War. The war held up the completion of the ideal for years, and it was not until the turmoil and stress of that period was well out of the way that the real impetus was given to the building or, rather, the completion of the Federal capital at Canberra. This is no place to review the many arguments for and against the establishment of the capital in that part of New South Wales, or, indeed, the much-discussed question whether Australia needed a new city at all, having within her boundaries such beautiful examples of the modern city as any of the six capitals of the states. The Australians had set themselves the ideal of having such a legislative and administrative centre as would be a monument to the Commonwealth sentiment, and very worthily have they embarked upon the carrying out of that ideal.

That sentiment of high emprise and high ideal could not fail to have its reaction in the King's attitude as he came nearer to his task. Moreover, he was coming to a country which, though still meagre of population, had within its borders far more millions than hitherto he had met. Sydney, for example, where the first landing was made, could boast a population within a fifty-mile limit greater than the whole of the population of New Zealand. And, indeed, the whole of that population seemed to be out on the headlands of Sydney's magnificent harbour or thronging the streets on the day of the

Royal arrival—a day of glorious sun, of brilliant blue and gold such as Sydney loves to offer its visitors. Having made their welcome manifest, the Sydney people never let their enthusiasm wane. Indeed, they became on occasion just a little too extravagant in their expression of affection—as when they stood in a solid mass round the dais in the Town Hall at the citizens' ball and just gazed fixedly at the embarrassed King and Queen sitting there until one of the stewards had to make a speech, begging them to dance and allow their guests to dance also. Even when they responded to that appeal the appearance of the King and Queen on the dancing floor was the signal for another rush, and the Royal couple had eventually to dance in the centre of a ring of stewards and other helpers who linked arms and cleared a space of about five yards diameter, a rather trying experience. Enormous crowds thronged the streets along every avenue where it was known that the King and Queen were to drive, and all the time of their stay in Sydney the public desire to see them never slackened.

It was at Sydney, too, that a new type of function was inaugurated, which was repeated at all the State capitals and also at Canberra. It was called in the official programme a " Public Reception," and its object was to give as many people as possible a " close-up " of the Royal pair. To that end they stood side by side on a low dais, while the public, eagerly seizing any opportunity of " sighting " the King and Queen, marched past in their thousands, sometimes four, sometimes eight abreast, without stopping, and carefully marshalled by the police so that there should be no undue delay. Of course there were in these receptions many unrehearsed and humorous incidents, as when in Hobart the last of all the people who " went past " in Franklin Park was a proud father wheeling a bonny pair of twins in a perambulator. Or again, in Adelaide, another pair of twins, this time a few years older, broke ranks to hand up to the smiling Queen a threepenny bit to " put in Princess Betty's money-box," where, no doubt, it still reposes. Then there were the irrepressibles who insisted on falling out and telling the King that they remembered when his father came out in *Bacchante*, or that they had been present when his grandmother [*sic*] arrived to marry King Edward. And there were always the flappers who carried cameras and tied themselves into all manner of complicated contortions in their efforts to keep on walking and at the same time snap the King and Queen from sideways on. In Perth this procedure was amusingly varied by a Girl Guide who established herself in the crutch of a tree right opposite and a few feet away from where the King and Queen stood in the public park. There she obligingly operated all the cameras her friends handed up to her. The King " spotted " her early in the proceedings and laughingly pointed out to the Queen one of her comrades in the Girl Guide Corps, obviously doing her good deed for the day. These receptions were crowded in every city, but the record must surely go to Sydney, where twenty thousand people went by in a densely moving river of humanity, and twice that number had to be refused admission to the Town Hall as time would not allow any further marching.

It is typical of the King's determination to keep abreast of Industrial Welfare conditions wherever he could find them that, on that same day, he made one of his characteristic dashes into the industrial area, to see some of Sydney's factories. He could well have been excused the effort. In the morning of the day in question—March 29th—as soon as the King and Queen had regretfully to agree to the closure of the public reception, the King had to hurry away to a lunch of Returned Soldiers and Sailors. In itself that was a memorable event, for Prime Ministers, Judges of the Supreme Court, Captains of Industry, Mercantile Clerks, and working men were all there, their only right of entrée being that they had fought side by side in the Great War. After the lunch there was a huge children's display, miles away on the other side of the city, and then a University function to round off the afternoon. Mercifully that night's dinner was a private one, but there was a gala performance at the chief theatre in the evening. Yet despite all this rush the King fitted in a visit to a tobacco factory and a woollen mill, where he inspected not only the " working parts," but more eagerly still the provision that had been made for the comfort and well-being of the workpeople. He was, moreover, continually meeting at the various functions men whose work or whose experiences interested him. He always tried to arrange that these men should see him quietly and privately at his own rooms in the various Government houses, where to the accompaniment of a good cigar they could talk across the table of the many aspects of labour and employment which invariably appeal to the King. It mattered not the political complexion of the visitor, less did it matter whether he happened to be a large employer of men, a pioneer who had battled his way to the front through years of fierce competition, or a man still working with his hands whose wide experience of conditions had made his views worth while. All were fish that came to the King's net and very readily did the Australian leaders respond to his mood and try their utmost to give him much from their store of experience. Indeed, there is no doubt that the multitudinous instances of this tendency in the King's character, this very obvious concern for the people's affairs, and this consideration— which the Queen shared to the full—for their well-being, is now one of the abiding impressions of the tour left with Australians. Mr. Charlton, the then leader of the Federal Labour Party and so of the official opposition, gave deliberate expression to the people's appreciation of this at the Federal banquet in Melbourne, when he told, quite emotionally, the story of the King and Queen's visit to Newcastle, the coal-mining city to the north of Sydney. " They arrived there in the drenching rain. Thousands of people stood in the downpour, and one thing on that occasion had endeared the King and Queen to the people. Immediately the King went to his car he decided to drop the hood. The King thought that if it was good enough for the people to come out in the drenching rain, it was good enough to give them a good view. The courtesy extended to the people by their Majesties had done much to cement more closely the bonds of kinship that existed with the Mother Country."

The lay-out of the Australian programme did not allow much time for country visits or indeed for very much in the way of relaxation. Australia is a land of magnificent distances, and such time as was not required for fulfilling the many engagements, official and semi-official, set down for the King and Queen was required for the purposes of transport from town to town. But advantage was taken of such opportunities as presented themselves for a few hours off duty. Their first Sunday was spent in the beautiful surroundings of Camden Park, one of the oldest estates in Australia, and the home of the Merino wool industry which is now the country's proudest boast, at any rate in the pastoral field. It was there, more than a century ago, that Captain John Macarthur turned down his first small flock of sheep—the gift curiously enough of " farmer George "—George III of England. The estate has remained in the possession of the family ever since, and Mr. James Macarthur Onslow was the King's host on this occasion. It is not to be imagined, though, that Camden Park is a typical Australian "run." A century of careful tending has made it more like an English park of great extent, with most of the characteristics of the homeland. Indeed the Queen's comment as they drove through it was, "This is like Home." The King, keen to get across a horse again, was soon in the saddle and spent the afternoon in a glorious gallop across country to the Camden agricultural show, where the usual enthusiastic reception awaited him. It was, however, reserved for Queensland to give him his first taste of sports and crafts that are racy of the soil, and it is worth recalling that it was in Queensland that His Majesty, King George V, first tasted the delights of a "billy tea," that alfresco picnic, where against a convenient log the picnickers rest and drink tea brewed, as it should be brewed, in a tin can that is called a billy. During their visit to Brisbane the King and Queen were taken fifty miles or so to Beaudesert, where they saw a programme much of which they could have seen nowhere else in the world. It was the day of the annual camp drafting championships and some of the best horsemen in Queensland were competing. The trials consist in each competitor "cutting out" from a herd of bullocks certain selected animals and "drafting" or driving them into a yard. Another trial is for each rider to take a bullock through a defined area much as a sheep-dog takes a sheep, man and horse working together with almost uncanny co-operation. Items

more of a " rodeo " nature were also on the programme, such as riding bullocks, buck jumping, and
so on. Still more Australian, however, was the
aboriginal display that followed. The Australian
aborigine is regarded as very low in the human
scale, but he has an extraordinary skill in the arts
of the chase and the battle. He can track better than
the American Indian could in the palmiest days of
Fenimore Cooper's heroes, and with the most primitive weapons he hunted and killed his meat or his
enemies alike. To-day such natives as could be
secured for the display were hardly of the real
savage. Most of them had acquired some of the
veneer of civilization and had spent many of their
years among or in contact with white folk. But the
old skill had not deserted them, and the King saw
a wonderful exhibition of boomerang and spear-
throwing. Almost naked, with their bodies weirdly
smeared with white and coloured clays, the blacks
indulged in a mimic battle, hurling spears and *nullah
nullahs* or clubs at each other with every disregard
for their comrades' lives and limbs. They also performed some of their *corroborrees* or tribal dances,
and the men gave two wonderful displays of throwing
accuracy. In the first, one of their number tore
round the arena towing behind him a full-sized
model in tin of a kangaroo which the others battered
into an unrecognizable mass with their clubs,
boomerangs, and spears from any distance up to a
hundred yards. Then one of the leaders took a
small shield of wood and stood out in the centre of

Central News

LANDING THE BIG GAME FISH IN NEW ZEALAND

Graphic Photo Union

THE KING ENJOYS A JOKE WITH THE BOYS AT HIS CAMP
AT SOUTHWOLD

the ground as a target for his fellows, who forthwith proceeded to hurl their spears at him. These he dodged easily, or if they came too close, turned aside with the shield with a flick of the wrist that was most dexterous.

It was a great day for the King and Queen, and indeed so interested was the King in the stock riding that he was up early next morning and out in the paddocks of Tamrookum station, where they were spending a week-end, determined to try for himself the sensations and thrills of drafting cattle. So they brought in a mob of bullocks, mounted the King on Elsinore, one of the champion stock horses of the district, and let him help in the whole process. For an hour or two he most thoroughly enjoyed himself, doing his full share of cutting out and drafting, and learning what it was like to be across a horse that most adequately knew its job and what was expected of it as a camp horse. "This is the life for a man," was his comment as he rode back to the station for breakfast. Later in the tour he was to have another typical Australian day. At the close of the Adelaide visit, the King and Queen spent a day on a South Australian station, "Wellington Lodge," on the shore of Lake Alexandrina. There the King had a great gallop after a deer which was lassooed and then freed, and later came the crowning "thrill" of all, a real "honest to goodness" kangaroo hunt, horses and dogs in full cry after a regular "boomer," which was eventually run down and captured in the boundary rider's style of leaning from the saddle, grasping the animal by the tail and throwing it. The Queen followed the hunt in a motor-car and the kangaroo was kept until she came up, photographed, and then allowed to go free.

It was at Melbourne that the first really serious note of the tour was struck. Two events combined to that end. The first was Anzac Day—April 25th —the most solemn day in the Australian calendar, more solemn even than Armistice Day, for it commemorates the landing at Gallipoli, the baptism of blood for Australians and New Zealanders in the Great War. On that day the King saw what was undoubtedly one of the most impressive demonstrations of the whole tour—the march past of some twenty or thirty thousand ex-service men, and the deeply emotional service in the Exhibition building which followed it. Men had come from all over Australia to take part in it and to salute their dead, symbolized in the temporary cenotaph which had been erected on the steps of Parliament House where also the King a few steps further on stood to take the salute. Ten abreast, marching with the swing and poise they had learnt in the mud of France and Flanders, or on the sun-drenched plains of Palestine, the river of men flowed on for an hour and a half, headed by their own battalion commanders, and their own battle colours. The sick and maimed and nurses led the procession and with them were twenty-nine winners of the Victoria Cross. In the rear were New Zealand comrades and veterans of other wars, the whole wonderful column ending with fifty

British ex-service men of the " Old Contemptibles." Some of the men in the march still wore their old and honoured uniform, but year by year the proportion of these grows smaller and smaller, and to-day nearly all the old Anzacs who take part in these recurring demonstrations are in civilian garb—in itself a fact that serves to emphasize the citizen-soldier character of the Australian troops. The whole affair was, too, the highest vindication of democracy. Side by side there marched a man high in the councils of the State and a tram conductor, a captain of industry and one of his junior clerks ; at the head of one division marched a judge ; the battle flag of another was born by a corporation labourer. Above all the pride of race that rhythmically flowing column inspired there rose, too, the harrowing thought that of all the men there that day, double the number had yielded their lives in the same cause, men of the best blood in Australia and therefore men that Australia could ill spare.

The other serious occasion that fell to Melbourne's lot was the Federal banquet in the Parliament House there, a Federal Parliament House that was soon to revert to its original function of housing the Parliament of the State of Victoria. That State had lent it to the Commonwealth when Melbourne became the seat of Government until the Commonwealth should have a home of its own. In the same building in which the banquet was held the first Federal Parliament, which had been opened by the King, had assembled ; it was there that all the legislation

of the Commonwealth had been passed in the
twenty-six years that had elapsed since that historic
occasion ; it was there that decisions were taken
which threw Australia into the melting-pot of war
from which she emerged a Nation indissolubly
welded by common suffering and common glory.
It was therefore peculiarly fitting, in the words of
the Federal Prime Minister, the Hon. Stanley Melbourne Bruce, now High Commissioner for Australia
in London, that one of the last acts of the Federal
Parliament which had worked in those halls so long
should be to do honour to the son of the King who
had so intimately been associated with the establishment of Federation. No more representative gathering had ever assembled in Australia since the day of
the Proclamation made by King George establishing
the Parliament. The speeches of the Prime Minister
himself, of Mr. Charlton, the leader of the Opposition, and more particularly that of the King himself,
reflected very fully the importance of the occasion.
In his speech the King struck again his favourite
theme — the absolute necessity of co-operation
between all classes.

" One of the great needs of to-day, and perhaps
the greatest need of all, is the better understanding
of one another, both between the different parts of
the Empire and also between the different interests
—Capital and Labour, employers and employed,
town and country—in the various countries themselves. It is only by getting to know one another
better that this closer sympathy and understanding

can come. Only so can we realize that we are all members of one family, whose interests are inseparably bound up with one another, possessing the same traditions, animated by the same ideals, imbued with the same faith. That is the message I would bring. It is right that we should be loyal to our family, to our city, to our State, to our country, but let us not forget the wider patriotism, the loyalty that we all owe to the British Commonwealth—that great family of British nations, in the preservation of which, and of the ideals and principles for which it stands, lies in my opinion the best hope of peace in the world to-day."

Let it not be thought, though, that the Melbourne visit was all serious. There were many lighter moments. For instance, the Melbourne University students staged for the King's benefit one of the most elaborate, as it was one of the funniest, " rags " of the whole tour. Throughout the visit there had been much complaint—some of it justified—that the country interests were being ignored for the sake of the cities and loud and long were the regrets that those who dwelt in the country had no opportunity of seeing the Royal party. So the students capitalized on that feeling and coining a slogan, " If the Duke can't go to the country, the country must come to the Duke," they met him on the day he visited the University with a most amazing collection of caricatures on the farming community, with livestock—cows, sheep, goats and draft horses—all complete. When the King arrived for his investment of

the degree of Doctor of Laws, he found a whole
company of students burlesquing the whole of the
Royal party, including one muscular specimen who
masqueraded as the Queen, and on his departure he
was enticed into an ancient landau in which he made
a tour of the grounds, the Royal procession being
completed by a still more dilapidated " jinker " and
a milk cart with the " Country Party " bringing up
the rear, its members and its bewildered sheep and
goats inextricably mixed up with the mob of wildly
cheering and hysterical students who swarmed everywhere. At intervals the procession pulled up for the
presentation of absurd addresses of welcome, strictly
unofficial, not to say familiar, in their language,
and finally the King, who was most thoroughly
enjoying himself, found himself somehow created a
Mayor. Thereupon he seized on the bulkiest of the
attendant students, appointed him Town Clerk on
the spot and ordered him to read the speech. As the
culmination of a riotous morning, the King was
admitted as a member of the Students' Club, made
an impromptu speech of thanks from the " dizzy
heights " of a chair and was allowed to leave to the
heartfelt strains of " For he's a jolly good fellow."
Another very democratic occasion was at the famous
Flemington race-course, where the King and Queen
spent an afternoon. Behind the stands of that
beautifully appointed course there rises " the Hill "
devoted to the more numerous and less wealthy
followers of the game. Half-way through the programme, the King and Queen left the Royal box,

and in their motor drove to another which had been prepared for them there, to the accompaniment of almost delirious enthusiasm from the huge crowd which packed the whole space. Indeed those crowds were a feature everywhere in Melbourne. Whenever the King and Queen went abroad there were thousands to greet them. One evening, when they were going to a reception in the Exhibition building, their car took nearly three-quarters of an hour to cover the two miles between Government House and the building where the reception was held—ordinarily a ten-minute journey. The crowd simply would not allow the car to go through—one of the most amazing examples of " undisciplined loyalty," as Lord Cavan termed it, of the whole tour.

After the Melbourne visit, which ended on April 29th, there remained only a brief visit to Adelaide before the culmination of the tour—the opening of the Federal Parliament House at Canberra—took place. The answer to the complaints—already referred to—from the country districts that they were not given their fair share of opportunities of seeing the King and Queen, is to be found in the fact that it took the excellently appointed Royal train, travelling at a high speed, from Friday afternoon to the Sunday morning to cover the journey between the two places—with only a few hours' break at Geelong and Melbourne as interruptions. And Canberra and Adelaide are cheek by jowl when compared to some of the places whose people thought that they ought to see the King and Queen. Time was altogether too short and distances too great to permit of any more than the brief dashes into the country which the King and Queen were enabled to make, sometimes at the cost of a very tiring and more than ordinarily busy day.

The stately ceremonial at Canberra was of the most inspiring description. Australians are to some extent popularly supposed to be impatient of old forms and hoary tradition, but for this occasion they had organized and carried out without a single hitch a peculiarly impressive programme. For pageant and ritual, of course, London is deservedly supposed to hold pride of place throughout the Empire—if not throughout the world. To those—and there must have been many such in the attendant crowds—who remembered a State opening of Parliament or a Royal progress through the City—it must have been strange to have the scene and the pageantry unroll before their eyes on that wide Australian plain with an autumn sun pouring its effulgence from a cloudless sky and, in place of bricks and mortar, avenues of trees just "from the nursery," between which the old-fashioned State carriages with the gaily caparisoned horses, outriders, and postilions complete, rolled cumbrously up to the broad, deep steps of the very "modern" Parliament House, as unlike as could be to the Gothic of Westminster, yet expressing something, very successfully, of the spirit of the place, the depth of distance and the far-flung panorama of rolling down and open plain. The ceremony itself, in keeping with the British instinct, was made as simple as possible. The King, a slight figure in the blue and gold of his naval uniform, wearing the insignia of the Grand Cross of St. Michael and St. George, and the ribbon of the Garter, stood at the head of the steps with the Queen and the Governor-General and Lady Stonehaven, with State and Federal dignitaries grouped round him. The crystal voice of Dame Nellie Melba pealed out the National Anthem, Mr. Bruce made a brief and dignified speech, asking the King to unlock the doors ; the King's reply was as short and no less solemn and inspiring. After that there remained the unveiling of the statue of King George V in the King's Hall and the actual declaration that the Parliament was open. This declaration the King made in the Senate Chamber, coupling with it a message from King George V, gracefully referring to the " day of happy memories " (for it was on May 9th, 1901, that he had declared open the first Federal Parliament, on the same day of the month as his son was opening the new Parliament House).

The day was further marked by a luncheon into which there were imported two features hitherto absent from all similar functions of the tour. In the first place there were no speeches, an innovation which must have been welcome to the King, and in the second place no alcoholic liquors were served, Canberra then being—officially at any rate —a " dry " town. It is, by the way, interesting to note here that since the Royal visit the capital has reverted, and by plebiscite the residents decided that they preferred to be wet. A good story went the rounds anent this luncheon. The Federal caterers who were responsible for the arrangements were not at all sure whether fruit juices and mineral waters would be to the taste of the King. So they thoughtfully provided something of a stronger nature should the Royal guest express a preference for it. But the King naturally declined as a guest to partake of anything different from the beverages of his hosts. So he asked quite innocently for soda-water. And it took quite ten minutes for the soda-water to be produced! The same day saw a most significant military review on the newly prepared parade ground. There three thousand men were assembled, drawn from all over Australia. Every regiment in the citizen forces had sent down a colour-party with its regimental colours and guidons, and according to a high military authority the display of these colours and guidons was the largest that had ever been seen in any part of the world. There were sixty-two King's colours, sixty regimental colours, and eighteen Light Horse guidons, all emblazoned with the battle honours won during the war. They represented a citizen army one hundred thousand strong, and afforded convincing proof that Australia meant to be fore-armed to defend herself against any aggression, an impression strengthened next day when the King saw a very fine body of military cadets at the neighbouring Duntroon College, where Australians train their own sons for service in their own army.

The Canberra visit over, thoughts turned naturally homeward again. The King and Queen left Australia after a brief visit to Perth and West Australia, conscious of having done their work most thoroughly, of having endeared themselves to many thousands of men and women, contact even of the briefest with whom had been a sheer delight for them. Not least significant were the many times repeated assurance to themselves that they had by their unfailing consideration, helpfulness, and profound interest in all they saw and heard founded still more deeply the structure of the British Empire. It had been a very strenuous time, and the King and Queen are not to be blamed for that, during the first few days after leaving Fremantle on the homeward trip, they gave themselves up almost entirely to a thorough rest. Their only distraction at that period was the astounding collection of wild stock they found awaiting them when they rejoined *Renown*. It is said that Australian birds have no song—a libel, of course—but they certainly have a screech, as the King found out from the motley array of parrots and cockatoos which had been given him and the Queen. These were hung in cages all along the deck just outside his cabin, and until familiarity made him immune the various conversations which went on from cage to cage must have somewhat disturbed his rest. Besides these birds there were various animals ranging in size downwards from a pair of wallabies, which needed the attention of several officers and ratings. The last effort, by the way, to add to their zoological collection was made at Mauritius on the homeward voyage, when only the most strenuous and secret endeavour on the part of the staff prevented the King and Queen from being presented with a giant tortoise of incredible age and weight. Fortunately the King did not hear about this until Mauritius was hull down on the horizon. Otherwise he might, in the kindness of his heart, have insisted on accepting it so that no one's feelings should be hurt. It was at Mauritius, moreover, that the historic mistake in printing was made, one of the many local papers reporting a day or two before their arrival that the " Colonial Secretary announces that Their Royal Highnesses cannot *stand* more than two days in Mauritius." The word should have been " stay." And while on this subject the delicious bit of unconscious humour perpetrated by the programme at Gibraltar might be added to the list. The evening of their departure from that port was enlivened by a band concert from a steamer which drifted slowly abreast *Renown* as the latter lay at anchor. The programme concluded with the stage direction :

" As *Renown* is about to move off—hymn, ' Now thank we all our God.' "

The voyage homewards from Melbourne was

marked by two or three outstanding incidents, in addition to the calls made at Mauritius, Great Hanish Islands (for oiling and painting purposes), Malta and Gibraltar. In the first place, four days out from Melbourne and before reaching Fremantle, *Renown* ran into one of the worst hurricanes even the Australian Bight had to offer, and for a day and a night she laboured at reduced speed through enormous seas, bigger, according to the navigator, than any he had ever encountered. Then a few days after leaving Australia there occurred perhaps the most exciting incident of the tour—the fire in the oil bunkers, which broke out when the ship was a thousand miles from any land and outside the regular traffic lines altogether. It might easily have turned into a disaster of the first magnitude had it not been for the superhuman way in which the engine-room staff and ratings worked to prevent it spreading. If they had not been successful there would have been nothing for it but to take to the boats, for *Renown* was fully loaded as to her magazines, and if the fire had reached them she would have gone up in one shattering explosion. There was a complete absence of anything approaching panic on board, however, a fact to which the calmness of the King and Queen did its contributory share. The King was down as near as possible to the seat of the fire very soon after it started, and all the afternoon was " handy by " in case there should be need of emergency help. These were practically the only outstanding incidents of the homeward trip, which finished as it began, at Portsmouth, with the King, as he has many times admitted since, the richer by the contacts and experiences of a very varied and very illuminating tour.

CHAPTER THIRTEEN

THE NEXT TEN YEARS

THE return of the King and Queen found their homeland eager to welcome them. Their arrival in London was greeted by huge crowds who thronged the streets from station to Buckingham Palace, and there, would not be denied the sight of the Royal couple on the balcony while the appearance of the Queen with the Princess Elizabeth in her arms was the signal for a wild outburst of cheering. It was not realized then that the journey was the last of the Empire tours that the King was to undertake. At times during the years that followed several rumours as to such tours were in existence, and at one time the quidnuncs were quite certain that he would be appointed a Governor-General of one of the great Dominions beyond the seas. But a variety of reasons kept him within easy reach of London, although he and the Queen made several trips abroad. Circumstances such as the birth of his younger daughter in 1930, the illness of King George at the end of 1928, were against him, much though his further visits to other parts of the Empire were desired. Now it is to be feared that his peoples beyond the seas will have to forgo the pride and the pleasure of seeing him, except, indeed, for his crowning at the Coronation Durbar in India at the end of 1937. But the early years of the present decade were filled for him and for the Queen with a quiet, painstaking work throughout the length and breadth of Great Britain, work wherein the King enriched his knowledge, widened his experiences, and based still more firmly that underlying love and popularity with his subjects which was to blossom forth so manifestly in the weeks immediately succeeding his accession.

His travels beyond the shores of Great Britain during this period may be briefly summarised. His visit to Norway in 1929 to attend the wedding of Crown Prince Olaf to Princess Martha of Sweden has already been mentioned. The Queen was with him, and everywhere there was the same enthusiasm as marked their triumphal tour through the Empire. It was while he was on this visit that he took the opportunity of making a diversion so as to take in Berlin and leave a card on President Hindenburg. Though quite informal and devoted otherwise to sight-seeing, the visit has its significance in being the first visit paid by an English Prince of the Blood to Germany since the war. The next year the King and Queen represented the Royal Family at the wedding of Crown Prince Humbert of Italy, Prince of Piedmont, to Princess Marie José of Belgium in Brussels. In 1931 the King and Queen went to Paris for the Great Colonial Exhibition there and were welcomed by large crowds. They saw again the African dances they had themselves seen during

Fox Photos

A FAVOURITE HOBBY

Fox Photos

POLO AT MALDON

their early married life, inspected the varied products of the French Colonial Empire, and in the evening were the guests of honour at a banquet, whereat the King proposed the toast of "the Franco-British Entente and the prosperity of France and her colonial Empire.

"Our two colonial Empires," he said, "adjoin all over the globe. . . . Our common frontiers, far from creating causes of dissension, encourage us towards an ever friendlier co-operation." They were in France later in the same year and attended a reception held in their honour by the Paris Municipal Council. The last foreign country to be visited by him before his accession was Belgium. He and the Queen flew to Brussels in July to visit the International Exhibition—it was the Queen's first flight in an aeroplane—and they were naturally the foremost figures in the great ball given in their honour in the British pavilion. Later in the year the King was to be in Brussels again on a far sadder mission—to represent the King, his father, at the funeral of Queen Astrid, so tragically killed in a motoring accident.

At home, as abroad, the King during the first eight years after his return from his Odyssey of Empire kept himself ever busy, occupied not only with the immediate affairs of State which claimed his attention and the many journeys he and the Queen made throughout the length and breadth of the land, but also in enlarging his contacts on all the fronts of his many ideals and enthusiasms. As has been mentioned, the illness of King George V in 1928 found him the only one of his four brothers in the country, and the duty of fulfilling not only the mournful task of attending on a sorrowing Queen but of answering the calls of the State inevitably devolved upon him. Two events in the two following years bound closer still the love and the affection of the Scottish people to him and to his Queen. The first was his appointment in 1929 to be Lord High Commissioner to the General Assembly of Scotland, which took him to Edinburgh for his enthronement. It was the first occasion on which a member of the Royal Family had attended since King James VI of Scotland had removed his court to London.

The visit was made still more important by the fact that it marked the reunion of the Established Church and the Free Churches after the disruption of 1843. This recalls another instance of the King's remarkable memory and his aptness in applying it. An old lady who remembered the events of that unhappy period was telling the King about it. He told her as a companion incident that when travelling through the Darling Downs in Queensland on his way to Brisbane he had stopped at a little farming town—Clifton—where he had met an old pioneer, Mr. Hinrichsen, a Dane, who had been one of the guard of honour to Queen Alexandra when she left Copenhagen for her marriage to King Edward VII. Now the train only stopped for an hour or so at Clifton and the time was fully taken up with addresses of welcome and so on, so that the incident could quite pardonably have slipped his memory. But it did not, and was there for its apposite use. The other event of peculiarly Scottish significance was the birth of the Princess Margaret Rose at Glamis Castle in August 1930. Not only was there a Scottish born princess, therefore, but the choice of the name Margaret for her roused special delight in northern hearts, for the name has had a long and unbroken association with Scottish Royal Families. The bonds then forged between the people of Scotland and their future King and Queen were to be further strengthened when King George V appointed the King to represent him at the Jubilee Celebrations in Edinburgh in 1935. It was as though the King had been recognized by his father as one having peculiar claims on the affection of his Scottish subjects. The King's ties to Scotland were further cemented in 1936 when he was nominated and installed Most Worshipful Grand Master of Scotland during the bi-centenary celebrations of the Grand Lodge of Scottish Freemasons in November. In the same month he was made a freeman of the ancient city of Edinburgh, an honour he shares with the Queen.

It would be an impossible task to chronicle here all the activities of the King and Queen during the years from 1928 to 1935. They were constantly occupied with visits to all parts of England, Scotland and Wales. Wherever they went they were greeted with the utmost enthusiasm, and wherever they went the King neglected no single opportunity of getting into touch with and finding the latest information about the varied aspects of his chosen subjects, particularly the welfare of the workers and the uplift of the younger generation. Throughout the Midlands and the North, at Tyneside, in Yorkshire, through the Lancashire industrial area, in the Black Country, he held dozens of conferences with employers in the interests of the Industrial Welfare Society, and beyond that made himself thoroughly familiar with the conditions of employer and employed in the highly industrialized centres of England which he visited. There is a typical incident during one of his tours of Lancashire. His programme included in one town an inspection of a factory where there was some rather interesting new machinery. This was installed on the first floor, and when the King arrived he asked to be shown this portion of the plant first of all instead of going through the ground floor part as had been arranged. The hands on the first floor were not told of the change in plan, and when the King arrived at the door of the machine room he was confronted by an array of backs crowding round the windows anxious to catch a glimpse of the Royal party. He made his inspection of the room, walked all round the equipment with his escort of experts, and departed before the men and women had realized that he was among them. Outstanding among the engagements of the period were the opening of the vertical bridge over the Tees at Middlesbrough—the first of its kind

in England—in 1924 and his presidency over the
Salvation Army's immense gathering to farewell
" General " Higgins on his retirement from the
leadership. At that gathering he paid a striking
tribute to the work of the Salvation Army and the
enduring claim that it had upon the regard of members of the Royal Family and " upon all sincere and
thoughtful people." With it all he found time for
relaxation, and in 1930 he played himself in as
Captain of the Royal and Ancient Golf Club with
a fine straight drive of 180 yards.

The year of the Silver Jubilee naturally found his
engagements much increased, and the extra burden
they entailed were accepted cheerfully and meticulously performed. Besides deputizing for King
George at Edinburgh, there were many other functions which fell to him to attend in connection with
the celebrations—such as, for instance, the Jubilee
Tribute of the Boys' Brigade at the Albert Hall in
May. Nearly three thousand boys, running in
relays night and day, had borne a silver baton over
2309 miles, timed to reach the platform of the
Albert Hall on a strict schedule, and there the
King was waiting to receive it. It was during this
period, too, that his interest in hospital work
became even more deep than it had been in the past,
to be even further intensified in the next year, when
he took over from his brother the presidencies of
several hospitals which his accession to the throne
had compelled him to give up. Several of these
presidencies were accepted by the King, who spent

many hours with the officials of them, studying the special conditions of each and all the complex problems of hospital management and hospital finance. One of the principal nation-wide movements for the cure of the ailing, in which he had always been most assiduous, was the British Empire Cancer Campaign. In one of his speeches at a meeting he attended as President he said : " Of the many activities with which I am associated I can assure you that the cause stands second to none in my heartfelt wishes that the cure of cancer, or even advance in the medical knowledge of that subject, may cause material abatement in its tragic consequences." His concern went very much further than this, however. It was on his direct suggestion that a campaign of intensive propaganda throughout the country has been inaugurated " so as to encourage the public when in doubt to go to their doctors for advice as early as possible." Another suggestion he made which has been since acted on with marked success was for an annual appeal to be made throughout the Empire on Empire Day in aid of the work of the Cancer Campaign Council. A third suggestion revealing anew his keen sympathy for the " mere uncounted folk " was that " some form of organization might be set up to help poor patients to attend the Radium Fund Centres for treatment, especially when they live some distance away. I submit to the Campaign that they and their branches might consider if steps could be taken to provide for speedy and free transport of such patients in the case of urgent need." It was in every way fitting that he should, in June of 1935, attend the opening of the new Middlesex Hospital, which has been in the forefront of the battle against cancer. He had laid the foundation stone seven years previously, and he had the gratification of hearing that on the day of the opening two gifts each of £50,000 had been made to the rebuilding funds.

Practically his last official act in 1935 was to represent his father at the Cenotaph service, the first omen that all was not well with King George V, although at the time it was thought by the people that the inclemency of the weather was all that had kept him from being there himself.

CHAPTER FOURTEEN

1936

THE year 1936 opened in sorrow with the death of King George V in January. His own grief must have been deep indeed, for of all the King's sons King George VI stood closest to his father, alike in affection and in temperament. But with that same self-effacement so characteristic of him throughout his life he sank those personal feelings in his attention to his mother in her affliction and in his support of his brother in meeting the great responsibilities so suddenly thrust upon him. No more moving incident in that time when King George V was lying in State in Westminster could be conceived than when the King, with his three brothers, stood each at a corner of the catafalque, heads bowed and arms reversed at the midnight hour in a last tribute to the father they had loved and the King they had honoured. Through all the sad ceremonial of those days the nation will ever remember the slim figure of King George VI moving through the streets with grave eyes and downcast head behind his father's bier from station to Westminster Hall, from Westminster Hall to Windsor, where in the Royal Chapel as his father went to his resting-place he stood close to his mother, watching her, concerned for her, loving her.

The last rites over, the last prayers said, the King turned himself resolutely to the many problems which beset the new reign. Not for himself. It was for his brother that he shouldered whatever burden was then laid on him, anxious only that whatever he might do would be for the lightening of the grievous cares of King Edward VIII and for the good of his country and of the Empire he had grown to love. There was indeed no thought of self, as there never had been in the whole course of his service to the public. Disinterestedly, with his whole heart in his work he stood behind the brother he loved so dearly, had loved so dearly since as care-free youngsters they had played and fought together with no inkling that one day they would both be faced with a choice that would have its repercussions round the globe. His one object was to help that brother. He was as far as it was possible always at his side, his constant companion when events threw them together, and there must have been a genuine communion of spirit between the two. It would be impertinent to intrude upon the sacredness of those private feelings, but the last days of a year so instinct with drama, so heavy with tragedy, has permitted the lifting of the veil by their own hands. No more poignant moment in the Prime Minister's speech announcing the abdication of King Edward VIII could be imagined than when in a voice shaken with emotion he read that pathetic little pencilled note from the man who was laying down his crown :

> THE DUKE OF YORK AND THE KING HAVE ALWAYS BEEN ON THE BEST OF TERMS AS BROTHERS AND THE KING IS CONFIDENT THAT HIS BROTHER WILL RECEIVE AND DESERVE THE SUPPORT OF THE WHOLE EMPIRE.

That was one brother's tribute to another spoken from the deep heart of affection. The response was speedy and its tone the same. In his first message to the Parliament and through them to the Nation and the Empire King George spoke thus :

> I HAVE SUCCEEDED TO THE THRONE IN CIRCUM-STANCES WHICH ARE WITHOUT PRECEDENT AND AT A MOMENT OF GREAT PERSONAL DISTRESS. BUT I AM RESOLVED TO DO MY DUTY, AND I AM SUSTAINED BY THE KNOWLEDGE THAT I AM SUPPORTED BY THE WIDESPREAD GOODWILL AND SYMPATHY OF ALL MY SUBJECTS HERE AND THROUGHOUT THE WORLD.
>
> IT WILL BE MY CONSTANT ENDEAVOUR, WITH GOD'S HELP, SUPPORTED AS I SHALL BE BY MY DEAR WIFE, TO UPHOLD THE HONOUR OF THE REALM AND PROMOTE THE HAPPINESS OF MY PEOPLES.

This is neither the time nor the place to recount the history of those tragic days which saw a crisis suddenly flare up, the like of which the country has not known for three hundred years. Bewildered, the people saw events of which they had no premonitory warning pass swiftly across the horizon of their days, saw a King of the greatest Empire the world has ever known lay down the sceptre and of his own free will surrender the almost intolerable burdens of kingship, saw another take up those burdens, strengthened in his determination by the solace and comfort the other had never known. It will be for future historians to sift out fact, apportion impulses, weigh motives. One thing is certain. No matter what the verdict, one figure will stand above reproach, above calumny, above any accusation of self-interest. Through the momentous events of those days King George VI moved with dignity and resoluteness. He must have realized early that his efforts to turn his brother from the path he had chosen were breaking against the rock of inflexible determination. He never wavered. All the considerations of chivalry, of love, of sense of duty to the throne, and to the people, must have been put before the Duke of Windsor with a high courage and a deep affection. Moreover, with a complete disinterestedness. Faced as he was with a completely unexpected prospect of suddenly becoming King, no tittle of that consideration affected his daily, hourly, efforts to bring things back to the smoothness of the allotted path. We have the testimony of all who were at his side during those days for that. With that knowledge in the hearts of his people, with that knowledge too in his own heart, he begins his reign sure of their sympathy, surer still of their love. How deep, how widespread is that sympathy and that love already King George has had ample proof.

The grave words of the Prime Minister announcing the abdication had hardly got beyond the crowded benches of the House of Commons before the people in the streets were flocking to 145 Piccadilly to cheer the new King and to welcome him traditionally with "For He's a Jolly Good Fellow," to push and scramble for a glimpse of the young Princesses, to show in a hundred ways throughout the land that the new King was a popular King. Diffident as he always has been, hiding any realization of his popularity behind the symbols of sovereignty he conceived he represented, it must have sent a glow of happiness to his heart to find how strongly he had builded the edifice of his own personality and his own popularity. And that glow must have been intensified when the messages of loyalty began to come in first from the provinces and then from the Dominions and Colonies until the remote pearl fishing station in Australia, the hunting lodge in Canada's great North-West, the heart of Africa, and the fringe of the Arctic, had all sent back to their King and Emperor the promise of their loyalty and the assurances of their love. It is, too, a revelation of the strength of the King's personal touch, to read in the messages which came back from those parts of the world he and his Queen have visited, a warmer note. None were perfunctory. But from Australia, from New Zealand, and elsewhere in the far-flung Empire which had known him in days gone by, there were underlying the official phraseology a sentence here and there, even a word or the turn of a phrase which seemed to say : " We knew this man, we have looked into his face, we have shaken his hand. And he knows our problems, understands our aspirations, appreciates our point of view. It is good."

There remain the voices of Church and State to vindicate the past and forecast the future. Speaking in the House of Commons on December 14th, in moving that an address be presented to His Majesty, offering the Loyal thanks of Parliament for His Gracious message, expressing their devotion to his Royal person and to Her Majesty the Queen, and assuring His Majesty of their conviction that his reign, under the blessing of Divine Providence, would safeguard the liberties of the country and promote the prosperity and contentment of his people, Mr. Stanley Baldwin, as Leader of the House and Prime Minister of Great Britain, said :

" This is the last of the formal occasions which attend the Accession of a Sovereign until his Coronation. His Majesty has sent us a Gracious Message in which he reminds us that the circumstances in which he has succeeded to the Throne are without precedent. It is customary on these occasions to speak of the deceased King. In this case that is not our duty. The circumstances are without precedent. I think that all I have to say

I said—and I think I spoke for this House and for the country—last Thursday and in the few observations which I made on the third reading of the Abdication Bill on Friday—and I propose to make but a few observations on the other subject to which we always devote ourselves on these occasions, and that is the new reign.

" His Majesty speaks of moments of great personal distress. I can assure the House that that is no exaggeration and no mere formal phrase. When the one who succeeds is a brother, with the ties of affection that always have bound these brothers, the occasion cannot but be one of poignant distress. But I have the honour of knowing the new King well, and I would tell the House—if they do not know it already—that what will endear him to his people, if he be not already endeared, is that more than any of his brothers he resembles in character and disposition of mind his father, whose loss we were lamenting eleven short months ago. He will bring to his great task that same devotion to duty. Whatever may happen to him no personal predilections of any kind will stand between him and what he conceives to be his first duty, and that is to fulfil his great task as King and Emperor.

" His whole heart will be devoted to this task, and I am confident that this House and the country, in these circumstances, will give him all the support for which he asks ; and all the support that a man entering upon those tremendous responsibilities needs at this time. So while we all of us here know that of all things, to preserve our Monarchy in its integrity, it is necessary to keep it from controversy, controversy political, or controversy of any other kind, I feel a profound conviction from all I know of King George VI that never, of his will, will controversy, whether political or otherwise, be raised in connexion with him."

Finally, let the Primate of all England, the Archbishop of Canterbury, speaking to the whole nation in a broadcast address on Sunday, December 13th, speak for the whole nation in their hopes for the future and their estimation of the new order.

" So much for the past, and now the future. The darkness of an anxious time is over. A new morning has dawned. A new reign has begun. George VI is King.

" You can readily imagine what it means to him to be summoned so suddenly, so unexpectedly, in circumstances so painful to himself—for he was bound to his brother by ties of closest affection—to face the immense responsibilities of Kingship. Sympathy with him there must be, deep and real and personal. But it passes into loyalty, a loyalty all the more eager, strong, and resolute because it rises from this heart of sympathy. It is this whole-hearted loyalty which, with one heart and voice, the peoples of this realm and Empire offer him to-day. He will prove worthy of it.

" He is frank, straightforward, unaffected. The 6,000 boys from our public schools and from the homes of working folk whom for the last fifteen years he has gathered in the comradeship of a summer camp know that he has been himself a boy among them. In varied fields of service—in the Navy, in the Air Force, in association with all manner of public and charitablecauses—he has gained a wide experience.

" He has made the welfare of industrial workers his special care and study. There is no branch of industry where he is not at home.

" In his visits with the Queen to Central Africa, to Australia and New Zealand he has studied the peoples and the problems of the great Empire over which he is now called to rule.

" He has high ideals of life and duty, and he will pursue them with a quiet steadfastness of will. He inherits the name, he will follow the example, of King George V, to whose memory let us offer now the homage of our undying affection and respect.

" No passage in the last message of the Duke of Windsor—as we must now learn to call our late King—was more touching than that in which he spoke of his brother's ' matchless blessing '—a happy home with wife and children.

" King George will have at his side the gentle strength and quiet wisdom of a wife who has already endeared herself to all by her grace, her charm, her bright and eager kindliness of heart.

" As for her dear children, I will only say that they are as delightful and fascinating as she was in her own childhood as I remember it over thirty years ago. Truly it is good to think that among all the

THE QUEEN'S FIRST FLIGHT
(to Brussels, 1935)

Fox Photos

EQUIPPED TO GO DOWN A DURHAM MINE, 1936

homes of the Empire—the homes from which all
that is best within it springs—none can be more
happy and united than the home of our King and
Queen.

" A King has gone. God be with him. A King
has come. God bless him, keep him, guide him now
and ever."

CHAPTER FIFTEEN

THE DAY'S WORK

THERE is a story told of the Duke of Windsor that comes in very appositely when the actual day-to-day tasks of either he or any of the Royal princes are under consideration. One day when he hurried out of his club to keep some official or semi-official appointment, he found two young gentlemen of a somewhat Red persuasion inspecting his car. As he stepped in one of the coming revolutionaries said to the other : " One of the idle rich, Bill, I suppose." Quickly the Prince leaned from the wheel. " Rich perhaps," he retorted pleasantly, " but hang it all, not idle." Then he stepped on the accelerator and drove away without waiting for a reply. That same comment could with equal truth and equal sincerity be made by the King, who has all through his life since he gave up the comparative obscurity of a naval career never once shirked the call to public duty, has given ungrudging service to the country and the people whenever they have asked him. As has been pointed out, the post-war period during which his elder brother made some of his most valuable tours to the various parts of the Empire threw far more of the work of the Royal Family on to the shoulders of the King.

This was more especially the case because his younger brothers were then not old enough to take their full share in the burden, as Prince Henry, the Duke of Gloucester, has in the last few years commenced to do, or as Prince George, later still, is doing now. Even so, it is worth recording that when King George V first fell ill at the end of 1928 the King was the only one of the four brothers who was in England. The Duke of Windsor and the Duke of Gloucester were " on safari " in East Africa and many weeks elapsed before they could be brought into close contact with Buckingham Palace again, the Prince after a record dash by train and cruiser and train again and the Duke through to the Cape and then home by liner. Prince George was with his ship in American waters and the whole responsibility of that very anxious period devolved upon Queen Mary and her second son.

Still, it can be said that since the King returned from his world tour a little more system was infused into the preparation of the " roster," so to speak, whereby the members of the Royal Family share out the many demands made upon their time. Each of the Princes has his own special preoccupations. The King's have already been indicated, and whatever may be required of him in other directions these special interests, such as Industrial Welfare and the Boys' Camp, never suffer. His appetite whetted by the contacts he had made with industrial magnates he soon developed another and very valuable method of furthering his ideals of closer contact among all

classes, those ideals which have already been quoted
more than once in this volume. He might, to put a
concrete case, meet someone at luncheon or dinner
whose life and experiences had a quality of novelty
or a man who has some pet project in view which
interests the King. He would be asked to call at
145 Piccadilly to talk the matter over further and
without the interruptions inevitable to a public
gathering. He spent many hours of his time in this
way, and it is safe to say that if he could help the
guest in any way on his path to the realization of his
ambition it was done, quietly, unostentatiously, and
without any public announcement of the fact. Or
perhaps men he met in New Zealand or Australia or
elsewhere on his tours would " come home " for a
trip that combined business and pleasure. They
called to pay their respects, and if the King thought
he could smooth the way for them in the objects they
might have in view, then a little informal meeting
between the visitors and the men that matter on this
side was arranged, again without any publicity being
given to the visit. This system which he evolved
was altogether apart from the usual official calls
which are noted nearly every day in the Court
Circular—underneath that stratum of formal duties
lay this other, and in a way more valuable (from the
view-point both of the visitor and the host), contact.
The men who called in this delightfully informal
way were drawn from all classes of society. A casual
list made out over an unidentified period of a few
weeks revealed the fact that in that time the King

THE DAY'S WORK

saw high officials of the Miners' Federation and of
the Mining Association of Great Britain, men who
had been in the councils of the Federation and had
sought fresh avenues for their activities elsewhere.
There were veteran trade union leaders who had
fought for Labour ever since the Labour Party had
had a separate entity, and following them up the
steps, so to speak, came big employers of labour or
representatives of huge capitalistic concerns, parlia-
mentarians and Ministers of State " dropped in for
a chat." An Industrial Relations Counsellor from
New York called a few days before an official of the
Industrial Court here. A leading journalist came to
tell the King all about an expedition he had made on
behalf of his paper, and the chairman of a committee
on Training for Salesmanship gave the King all the
latest developments in this new effort to make the
commercial life more of a real profession than a job.

There is besides his pleasant study at 145 Piccadilly another favourite place where the King loved to
meet people and that was at the annual Boys' Camp
at New Romney, where the informality was even
more pronounced. There came to see the work of
the camp and to meet the founder and the moving
spirit of it, all sorts and conditions of men. A list
of these men would show the names of well-known
authors and press men, publishers and proprietors
of great newspapers, trade union leaders. Always
these representative men were welcome wherever
they saw the King, so too were the men whose names
as captains of industry are known wherever the work

213

of the world goes on. With these were mingled headmasters of famous schools and principals of State schools, philanthropists interested—as who is not ?—in the whole movement, and men from distant parts of the world anxious to see the scheme repeated in their own country. They met the King and each other on an absolute equality. Provided they could manage it they were perhaps more welcome if they donned pullovers and shorts than if they appeared in the more ordinary attire of conventional life, but they were welcome anyway. They watched or joined in the sports, talked with the boys and with the King all day, or sat round the camp fire and enjoyed the sing-song in the evening. And always there was the King ready to tell them more about the whole scheme or to listen to them while they expound their own ideas or outline what they have seen being done on the same lines elsewhere.

It must not be imagined, however, that these informal talks and contacts were of greater importance than the more official visits ; it was only that in them was provided another and friendlier means for the King to get at the heart of things and arrive more quickly at a closer appreciation of the subjects that matter in his world. The more formal calls at 145 Piccadilly yielded just as wide a field of information. There, as the Court Circular recorded from time to time, he was visited by Ambassadors and Foreign Ministers, by delegates summoned here to attend world conferences such as Medical and Cancer Campaign Congresses or the more localized Conference of the Early Closing Association. A French Field-Marshal—Maréchal Lyautey—was asked to call and tell him all about the campaign in Morocco. As soon as the New South Wales football team arrived in England they were told that the King would like to see them. One of the first visits paid by the Australian Economic Mission when it returned from its trip to Australia was paid to the King, and with them he compared experiences and impressions and " checked up " on the deductions he himself had made on his own tour through that country. Trade commissioners from Australia and New Zealand, indeed from any of the Dominions, were always bidden to bring the King their latest news of commercial developments in their own particular spheres, and State officials, especially those with whom he had come in contact during his tour, were summoned for the same purpose. Nor is the list of visits confined to his own countrymen. Even from as distinctive an American locality as Dayton, Ohio, there came to see him the President of the National Cash Register Company, while from the heart of the financial centre of the new—and perhaps of the old —world representatives of the Industrial Finance Corporation talked to him long and earnestly. But then the tale could go on indefinitely. Enough has surely been said to reveal to what numberless facets of the life of the community the King's gaze is constantly turned.

With so many different threads to keep him occupied, it has become inevitable that the King's daily life usually falls into certain well-defined schedules. Normally his day, when in London, begins before ten o'clock with the reading of the daily newspapers. At ten he is at work with his staff, and from then until noon he is very closely employed with them, discussing the heavy mail bag, arranging for future engagements, going over points in speeches he is to deliver, attending to his own private correspondence, and receiving visitors, either officially or informally, some of the many the nature of whom has been referred to already. At noon his wife claims him for a stroll before lunch, and their familiar figures were often seen in Hyde Park or Green Park or " window shopping " in Bond Street or Piccadilly. Indeed, their walks abroad on these occasions were of a far less noticeable character than those of their adored daughters who, when they take their airing, demand a carriage and attendants as well as a crowd of worshippers outside the door to watch them go forth. Whereas their parents, slipping out unobtrusively, were almost unnoticed, and if noticed were left unworried by the unwelcome attentions of the shopping crowds. They loved to turn in to a shop here and there on their excursions—as indeed do all the members of the Royal Family—and buy across the counter as ordinary customers, and if they could escape into the street again without being addressed as " Your Royal Highnesses " so much the better pleased were they. After luncheon, timed for half-past one, there was usually, especially in the season, some function for the King and Queen to attend, either together or, as often happens, he to one and she to another. If there were no engagements of this character, the King tried to get a little exercise, tennis perhaps, or golf, with hunting in the winter if he could find a meet near enough to London. Afternoon tea is always a family gathering, for then " the babies " come down, and until bedtime the four of them find perhaps the happiest hours of their day together. If there were no dinners to be attended in the King's capacity of " His Royal Highness," or as a private friend with one of their large circle, then the King and Queen dined quietly at home shortly after eight o'clock. The rest of the evening was spent according to their own inclinations. If they went out it was to a theatre or a cinema, where seats were kept for them on a telephone call as in the ordinary way, and occupants of the stalls without any previous warning would find the King and Queen passing to their seats with the rest of the theatre-goers. Indeed it was not always the stalls, for if the theatre was crowded and seats were all booked the King and Queen were quite content to have places found for them wherever a vacancy offered. If there were no theatrical attractions to tempt them out there might be a small dance at a friend's house. While it cannot be said that the King enjoys dancing as much as do his brothers, still he does occasionally like a turn on the polished floor, more particularly since his marriage and the kindly education the Queen has afforded him in the matter of the modern steps. Failing any

" outside attraction " the King and Queen are more than content to sit quietly at home, the King reading or—must it be confessed ?—doing cross-word puzzles, for he has become devoted to that most irritating of evening amusements.

That programme comprised a day which the wheat broker would describe as F.A.Q.—fair average quality. Contrast it with what the King would pack into the same number of hours when he was on one of his many expeditions into the provinces on some official mission or other. Then it seemed to be a point of honour with him to fill as many engagements as is humanly possible so that everybody who wanted his help in the opening of institutions or the further-ing of welfare projects or any other public activity might not go disappointed. Everybody who follows his movements at all will realize this. Here, for example, is the list of engagements he fulfilled in one day in Liverpool some little time ago, as Presi-dent of the Industrial Welfare Society. Getting into Liverpool early in the morning, he visited two large manufacturing concerns where he not only thoroughly inspected the machinery and plant, but paid even more attention to all that had been done for the benefit of the employees in the way of rest rooms, canteens, and so on. From there he went on to a Boys' Club to open an extension and to chat awhile with the committee and the boys themselves. A civic luncheon was next on the programme, and he spoke on the advantages of Industrial Welfare at that and praised the part Liverpool employers were playing in its furtherance. The luncheon over, he went straight on to a specially organized reception, where three hundred workpeople thoroughly representative of the city's industrial and commercial life had been invited. He went about among them, talked with them, and paid them all the compliment of staying until the last moment before his train left. That same evening he was in London speaking at some City banquet. A day like that could be duplicated—or multiplicated—over and over again from the record of the King's journals and diaries. The best illustration of how he travels about the country and the vast number of miles he covers is provided by a large-scale map which used to hang in the offices at 145 Piccadilly. On it the points visited by the various members of the Royal Family were marked with distinctive discs. Since his return from his world tour the King confined his travels mostly to the British Isles, but one notable journey he made abroad was his visit in March 1929 to Norway, with the Queen, to represent His Majesty King George V at the wedding at Oslo of the Crown Prince of Norway to Princess Martha of Sweden. Throughout the festivities there both he and the Queen enjoyed the most exceptional popularity. On their way to Oslo it was necessary for them to pass the night in Berlin, and though the visit was kept a purely private one the King can claim to be the first English Prince to have seen the German capital in its latest post-war development.

In all these myriad duties up and down the world

the King has fulfilled to the utmost the Shake-spearian adage which Jacques enunciates. In fact, he might with every justification lay claim to that title, " Protean," which was once such a favourite with music-hall actors who wanted to impress the public with the fact that they could play all the parts there were. To-day the King can claim personal experiences which entitle him to be classed in a huge variety of trades and professions. Of course, he is a Freeman of scores of cities and therefore ranks with the members of the guilds of Elizabethan times. Moreover, he is actually a Shipwright, a Draper, and a Fishmonger, having been admitted to the membership of those City Companies. He is a Druid and the Queen is a Druidess as the result of having incautiously accepted an invitation to attend the Swansea Eisteddfod, though perhaps the Druids do not insist that in the case of their distinguished comrades all the obligations required of the order shall be observed. He told the members of the Hardwicke Society once that though he was a Bencher of the Inner Temple he was not a Judge, but at any rate he is a Doctor of Laws of Melbourne, Sydney, Adelaide, and other Universities in Aus-tralia and New Zealand, and a D.C.L. of Oxford and Cambridge. He can operate quite adequately both the Monotype and Linotype, and can in addi-tion say that he has carried through other functions of the printer. These would come all the easier to him because he prefers to type his speeches and his notes himself rather than dictate them. A portable typewriter is always among his baggage and a more substantial one is at his elbow when he works at home. He has been a Civil Servant, and besides being an officer in all three Services, with a period of active rank in two of them, he is also a Boy Scout. His predilection for the mechanical side of life is found in the fact that he is always eager to get his hands on the controlling levers of any sort of machinery that he may come across in his industrial tours, and nothing delights him more than to get into the cab of a locomotive and feel the big monster move under his touch. When he brought the Royal train over the divide of the Southern Alps of New Zealand and down into the Canterbury Plains he hit a speed on the three-foot-six gauge that made the supervising engineer in the saloon behind look rather anxious once or twice. As to moving the engines through yards or down to their buffers, he has done that so often that it contains no further thrill for him.

On the more exotic side of life he can expect homage both as a Fiji and a Maori chief. The insignia of the former lies on his table at home in the shape of the huge whale's tooth tendered to him as a mark of fealty when he visited Suva, and the habiliments of the other, a cloak of kiwi feathers and flax mat with headband of the sacred hua feathers, rest in tin-lined cases. Then he has been a film actor with the ghastly green make-up on. When the Safety First Association decided that the best way to appeal to the children was by means of a movie the King came down to the studio where it was being made and went through all the business, playing his part under the glare of powerful arc lamps to the tune of the impertinent clicking of the cinema camera. The King showed all the characteristics of the movie star by refusing to play as the producer suggested, so that his work might be lessened. Instead he insisted on playing it as he would have done in real life. He was filmed looking at the medals awarded to drivers who go for long periods without an accident and also signing and handing to the late Sir William Joynson-Hicks—as he then was—a letter praising their achievements. All this he did just as he would have done if it had been at his own desk, and more than once he interrupted the action while he went over again a " bit of business " to make sure of getting it quite right. Perhaps the experience may account for the fact that he now carries with him wherever he can a movie camera of his own with which he has taken a very fine moving record of his travels everywhere and especially of " the babies." Perhaps also this " professional " appearance enabled him, as he did, to come to the rescue of the *Renown* operator when the machine broke down utterly in the middle of the Atlantic during a quarter-deck performance, and no one could get the thing to work again until the King had tendered his advice. And not only in the cinema line has he shone. Tradition has it that on one unforgettable afternoon he stood in the prompt corner of the

Hippodrome during some matinée or other and worked the scenes from that exalted spot sacred to the presence of pukka Stage managers—ambition can climb no dizzier heights.

There remains one more category in which to class the King. We have seen him as a not negligible member of city guilds and trade unions, though not perhaps with his card. We have seen him as an Officer of His Majesty's Forces ; we have seen him as a working member of the theatrical profession. The law, mechanics, skilled crafts, philanthropy can all boast that he is one of their number. The year 1929 his many duties invaded the Church also, and on the appointment of His Majesty the King, he became Lord High Commissioner of the Church of Scotland, a high dignity which involved residence for some days in the Palace of Holyrood House and attendances at several important meetings of Church dignitaries. From all this survey there is no doubt that whatever may be the demands made on his time and his devotion to public duty alike they will be met with the same sincere desire for public service, the same unstinted determination to give his best to that service.

CHAPTER SIXTEEN

THE SPORTSMAN

HARD as he works, the King plays just as hard. His boyhood years at Sandringham and the honest rivalry of two brothers almost of his own years, the anxiety of both his grandfather and his father that he should be equipped in all things as an English gentleman and sportsman, reacted to the utmost on a nature that was responsive to all the attractions of outdoor life. His training in field sports and in the national games went on side by side with his studies all through his younger years when he was under the guidance of Mr. Hansell and the other members of the teaching staff ; and when he went from there to Osborne and Dartmouth the love of games became intensified, as with all young naval officers. Whatever the season of the year, the King found something that attracted him. In winter it was football, and it is on record that whatever the knocks he took in that most strenuous of all games, he took them with a cheery smile, and was up and into the scrum again with the best. Fishing, shooting, and sailing were perhaps more to his taste for summer sports than cricket, but gradually his favourite pastime crystallized out of all this and he took up tennis far more

THE KING SHAKING HANDS WITH DISABLED
MEN AT STAMFORD BRIDGE

A KEEN GOLFER

assiduously than cricket. He became a very good left-handed player and figured in many of the summer competitions round London and elsewhere in the years immediately following the war. Playing with Miss Peggy Bouverie (now Mrs. Ingram), he won the mixed doubles at a big Charity Handicap in Highgate, and was more than once a competitor in the Service Championships at Queen's Club. In 1920 he won the R.A.F. doubles with Wing Commander Sir Louis Greig as his partner. The same pair were entered for the Wimbledon championships in 1926, but they were put out of the Men's Doubles by that redoubtable couple A. W. Gore and Roper Barrett. The event brought out one more instance of the King's diffidence in the way of seeking the limelight. The Wimbledon Committee, anxious, naturally, for a high light to attract spectators, wanted to stage the match on the Centre Court as an added " draw " for the meeting, but the King insisted on taking his due place on the roster and refused to be treated in any way above his deserts as a player. Few people perhaps have played tennis in more parts of the world than he has, from Wimbledon to Uganda, where during his trip to East Africa he played on a court laid out so that the centre line was directly on the Equator. Consequently whenever the King changed over he " crossed the line "—and still when Neptune boarded *Renown* he insisted on the King being ducked! Even after the most strenuous day of official duties and travelling during the world tour

he would if at all possible snatch time for a few
sets. Thus at Napier, a most tiring day in the train
did not deter him from hastening on to the Club
Courts as soon as the civic receptions were over for
a few sets with the New Zealand champion, or doing
the same thing in Melbourne with that erstwhile
wizard of the racquet, Norman Brooks—with whom,
by the way, arrangements were very nearly completed for the King to partner at Wimbledon in 1929.

If he could not get tennis, as was impossible on
the long voyage out to Australia, he compromised
on a sort of deck tennis, not only the ordinary type
with a quoit pitched over a high string net, but
another kind where the usual racquet was used and
the balls hit against a wooden framework under a
set of rules which every team of competitors
interpreted as it suited them. Far more to his liking
—miraculously enough considering the conditions—
was a hard game of squash-racquets in the wooden
court which had been built for a previous tour of the
Duke of Windsor, and, slung inboard just amidships
on the upper deck, haunted the soul of the commander by its unconcealable ugliness. It was a
dungeon about twenty or thirty feet square, with
no (or very little) ventilation, and exposed all
day to the directly vertical rays of the tropic sun,
the temperature in the interior was absolutely
terrifying. Yet the King and his ward-room
partners would put in an hour or more of a real
hard go. Once or twice they attracted the lazier
members of the ward-room mess to watch them,

but it has never been recorded that any one of these sybarites ever had the endurance to see the game through to its bitter end. On the other hand, the King would turn up in the ward-room apparently unharmed and chaff the weaker members with their lack of stamina. There was still another boardship game he affected which was even more athletic than squash-racquets, though the fact that it was played on the quarter-deck in the open air somewhat mitigated its rigours. This was deck hockey, a game that has no rules at all as far as a close study from a safe vantage point could discover. It consists for the most part of beating an unoffending grummet up and down the deck with walking-sticks until the grummet goes overboard or disintegrates. No respect is paid to the shins of the other side, and collision of bodies in violent motion with awning stays, gun turrets, ventilators, and deck bosses are considered all part of the game. It is a variety of deck sport much affected by the gun-room and junior watch officers, especially those whose contour is beginning to thicken, and though the King had no apprehensions in this regard he played several games during the course of the voyage.

While tennis still has his affections it is to be feared that the insidious charms of golf have worked their spell on him, and of late he has given far more attention to the game his brother, the Duke of Windsor, has always favoured. The King's handicap is yielding to intensive treatment until he can claim to be among the middle markers with every possibility of further improvement.

To all sport that has to do with horses the King is deeply devoted. He plays a very sound game of polo indeed, with keen eye and sound judgment, and at Malta at the end of his long voyage, fresh off the ship when land legs need not have been expected, he astonished everyone there by the excellent showing he made. He is very fond of hunting, and whenever he can get away during the hunting months he is pretty certain to be found at one of the meets, even if he has to pull out before the run is over in order to keep an afternoon or evening engagement in London. There is nothing he likes better than a good gallop over turf, and he was all the better able to cope with the unceasing demands on his time in Australia and New Zealand by the fact that he was now and again able to leave Government House before breakfast and get across a horse for an hour or so. On one such occasion in Melbourne some of his new-found friends arranged that a good steeplechaser should be waiting for him on the Caulfield race-course, and he took him round with every sign of pleasure. On another occasion he watched the early morning trials of racers and clocked alongside them for part of their gallops.

As has been said, the King was well grounded in the contemplative man's recreation, and the love of it has never left him. He is all for the rigour of the game too, as a good fly fisherman should be, and when he was given the chance of getting some of the monster trout that Lake Taupo in New Zealand yields to the troller, he preferred instead to keep to the more orthodox fly in the stream, though thereby he knew the fish that came to his gaff would be fewer and smaller. Again, at the other end of the Dominion he spent one whole day on Lake Wanaka with a biting autumn wind blowing off the first snows of winter for a reward of two fingerlings. Still, on that day he was only human, and the opinion he expressed of the day's sport when he returned cold and hungry to the hotel at Pembroke was not very flattering to the place as a fishing resort. But the language he used then was not a circumstance to the winged words he addressed to the Press photographers at the Bay of Islands. They had chartered a specially fitted launch to keep as near to the King as possible, and when they saw him fast to a two-hundred-pound fish they sheered in to get as good a close-up of the event as possible. Very natural perhaps—but so was the King's admonition to them when in simple sailorly language he told them to clear out and give him room so as not to let the hard-fighting shark get under their keel and saw himself free. Those who heard the address say they had never heard the King so inspired. There is a good trout stream at Glamis Castle, and though the sport there is perhaps not so exacting as it is in the newer countries, the King never fails to try his luck whenever he and the Queen spend any time there.

As with fishing, so with shooting. Into that sport he was initiated so early that he was probably not much higher than a full-sized breech-loader when he was first taken into the coverts round Sandringham and watched his father and grandfather at the sport they both loved so well. The keepers and his tutor saw to it that the young King missed no opportunity of improving his shooting and of increasing his experience of field game. Every holiday that was spent either at Sandringham or at Balmoral, or rather at the houses near by, the King had quite a respectable amount of shooting. He is almost, if not quite, as good a shot as his father was—there could be no higher criterion and he has the same shooting style as King George V. The love of it has continued always with the King. It would be hard to say which variety of shooting he likes best—the comparative comfort of covert shooting or behind butts or, on the other hand, the discomfort almost always inseparable from the pursuit of wild game— big or little—in their native haunts. At any rate, in whatever part of the world he has been he has consistently endured all the drawbacks and has felt himself amply rewarded when he has brought back a fair allowance of good specimen heads. All through the holiday tour in East Africa he devoted himself as far as he could to the hunting of the native fauna, and his walls are enriched with many a fine head which then fell to his gun. The world tour did not offer many opportunities for a day's shooting, but there were two occasions at least which must still remain, because of their novelty, in the King's memory. During his stay in Mauritius there was organized in his honour a day's sport known to the residents of the island as "La Chasse." Mauritius abounds in deer, the descendants, it is thought, of a herd introduced by the Dutch when they owned and cultivated the island in the seventeenth century. The deer were brought from the East Indian possessions of the Dutch and throve amazingly, so much so that one of the supporters of the Mauritian coat of arms is the local deer. They feed in herds through the low scrub that covers much of the island where it is not under sugar-cane, and as they are harmful to crops, as deer are in all parts of the world, the sportsmen have these elaborate deer drives very frequently through the season. The *modus operandi* has through decades of the sport been brought to a system. The local peasants are always ready to turn out as beaters, sufficiently rewarded with a share of the venison at the end of the day. They drive the deer through the brush towards a long line of butts that stretch across a wide strip of land, cleared of everything but grass. Some of these butts are elaborate affairs of concrete, others just a hole in the ground. As the deer break cover they are shot at with rifles from the butts, and it is a good shot that can bring down one of them as they swiftly cross in front of the butts, more particularly when summer sun has scorched the surrounding foliage to almost the same hue as the deer's hide. It is interesting to recall that the day's shooting was arranged by the

son of the planter who had been responsible for
" La Chasse " which had been held in honour of
King George V when he and Queen Mary visited
the island in 1901.

But the most infernal—the word is used advisedly
—experience of the whole tour must have been the
King's lot at Great Hanish Islands, where *Renown*
stayed to oil and paint. Great Hanish Islands are a
group of dreadful-looking volcanic peaks rising from
the Red Sea about a hundred miles north of Aden,
a rubbish-heap of useless rock and scoriæ and sands
washed by the sluggish sea which throws up on the
odorous beaches all sorts of marine filth. The tropic
sun—the islands lie in about 13° north latitude—
pours down unceasingly and the heat seems to gather
power as it is thrown back again upwards from the
ground. No one owns the place, no one wants to
own it, and no one ever goes there except a few
Arabs in search of shell-fish or one of the biggest
of the King's ships in search of a port that does not
charge harbour dues. How anything ever finds it
possible to live in the horrible place is inexplicable,
but a few gazelles do manage to eke out a precarious
existence on the extremely scanty herbage. It was
in search of one of these that the King landed,
deserting the comparative—very comparative—coolness of his quarters in *Renown* for a stalk through
this miniature reproduction of Hades. It must have
been almost unendurable agony, that stalk, all
among the red-hot rocks and across the sizzling
sands. But the King stood it, and his reward was a

head, and of a species very rare. That seemed to him quite sufficient compensation.

Though he has not yet followed in his father's footsteps to the extent of owning and racing his own yacht, the King is also very fond of sailing, and early in his naval career showed great handiness in charge of boats, both under oars and specially when as midshipman he had to take his own cutter under sail in the many exercises ordained for the further experience of the young officer in seamanship. Rowing he has never taken up seriously, but of course the University boat race finds him a loyal supporter of the Cambridge crew, and he early demonstrated his interest in the newest water sport of outboard motor-boat racing by donating a cup for yearly competition. As to other sports in which he takes a keen if non-active interest, the list of these would contain practically all the headings of any sporting symposium. He always manages to find time to see the more important football matches in both Rugby and Association codes, and athletic meetings also have their attraction for him. As for racing, it is hardly necessary to mention that he follows this as closely as his brothers do. He has ridden in point-to-point steeplechases, and though he has not " worn silk " on the flat he can at any rate boast of having officiated both as the starter and as the judge at a race meeting. That was in Christchurch during his tour of New Zealand, and a very enjoyable afternoon he made of it for himself. As to the more " fancy," or perhaps one should say "exotic," sports to be met with in journeying up and down the world, the King has always shown himself eager to try anything new, and mention has already been made of his day with the cattle at Tamrookum in Queensland and his gallop after deer and kangaroos in South Australia. Taken for all in all he can claim that, except for some purely "local" variants which he has not had the opportunity of testing, there is hardly a branch of sport in any category about which he has not some knowledge, and that knowledge is accompanied in the vast majority of cases by a thorough practical experience.

CHAPTER SEVENTEEN

A CHARACTER SKETCH

SOMEONE with a greater desire to invent a slogan than to preserve accuracy once described the King as " King George's serious son." There could be no greater misnomer. No one who knows the King would ever admit that the description comes within reasonable measure of his real character, which is that of the typical Englishman. He does not make friends very easily, preferring to subject those whom he meets to a testing period, that he may see whether they are really congenial. He meets all men and women with the same frank pleasure he always shows in contact with his fellows, but there is that touch of reserve so natural to the Englishman which, while it does not in any way repulse, at any rate discourages a precipitate advance into the closer bonds. Added to that natural reserve there has been until late years at any rate the unfortunate handicap of his hesitation in speaking which has, as can readily be understood, rather held him back from getting on to friendly terms too quickly with those he meets. The difficulties he has met with in speaking have engendered a diffidence in opening or in continuing a conversation, and thus the impression—a most unfair one—has been created that he is serious-minded and disinclined for friendship.

Once the barriers are down though there is a very different man to be met. He makes a delightful companion, easy and unaffected, with the faculty of inspiring affection. It is always a fresh pleasure to watch how liking for him grows, and how while the Queen with her radiating charm captures the heart at once the King, making his impression more slowly, nevertheless at the end of a public visit or a stay in any town invariably wins as much of the popular approval as his Queen held from the moment she appeared. Perhaps he has not the actor's trick of "projecting his personality" across the footlights, but the liking, the affection he inspires, has more lasting qualities, and his personality stays longer and more pleasantly in the memory for just that one reason. Then, too, he has always been very proud of the position he holds and very resolute to do nothing that would in any way detract from his high office. It was a splendid example of dignified aplomb to which he treated the Australians when he, as the King's appointed representative, opened the Federal Parliament at Canberra, perhaps the most important task that had, up to then, been entrusted to him. It was obvious that he felt very deeply the solemnity of the occasion, and he and the Queen both moved through the many ceremonial observances of the day with quite the right touch of regal poise, a different attitude altogether from that on the more light-hearted days of the less exacting portion of the tour.

But though he insists that his position shall be treated with the respect that is its due, he himself is very averse to ostentation in any shape or form. Readers of this book will remember the examples of this trait that have been quoted, the quiet visits to factories, and the departure, sometimes before the employers have had a chance of realizing that they have been entertaining Royalty unawares, the variation of official programmes so that he should see for himself and under no restrictions of formality what he had " come out for to see," the numberless instances where consideration for the public in general or the occupants of an institution in particular has caused him to see that their comfort or their convenience was more closely studied. Residents in London will treasure many memories of seeing him with his Queen strolling through the Parks that abut on Piccadilly or through the shopping centres with nothing to distinguish them from the crowds of other shoppers—that charming unconventionality which they share with other members of the Royal Family. There is, too, their habit of setting out for a theatre or cinema with no more preparation than the precaution of ringing up for seats at the show they most fancy.

As is well known, the King is extremely fond of reading, and his library, an extensive one, is always having additions made to it. In literature his tastes are catholic, and his study table will carry the heavy-looking tome last issued on some aspect of political or social economy side by side with the newest best seller among sensational novels. In other forms of art he would be the first to deny that his predilections are profound, but he has a sound preference for the lighter forms of music, and his gramophone albums and pianola cases are well stocked with other records than those of jazz dancing tunes. His choice of theatrical fare would lie in the direction of good musical pieces of the lighter order or comedy and farce—in short, for just what the young Englishman of his day and era, untroubled by any highbrow obsessions, would express a preference. When he is opening up a new subject, particularly one of those in which he is specially interested, he makes a point of " getting up his brief," so to speak, and if he has to make a speech it can safely be asserted that he has absorbed a great deal more detail than he has been able to make use of in his uttered words.

Over and above all, though, the one great attribute which has endeared him to all who have passed beyond the first barriers of his reserve is the spirit of youthfulness which surrounds him. Those who had the privilege of being with him on his voyage round the world carry many most delightful remembrances of this characteristic. There was, for instance, that evening in the Marquesas harbour when, tired with the long trek across the tropical Pacific, the King and Queen with some of the younger members of their staff went ashore in the cutter and bathed from the beach below R. L. Stevenson's bungalow, afterwards indulging in a regular romp on the sand. There was more than a spice of danger in the escapade, for sharks were by no means unknown in the harbour, but the cutter lay off-shore a little way and the big searchlight from *Renown* played on the laughing, happy group on shore all the time. The day *Renown* crossed the line has, with its initiation ceremonies in the morning and the elaborate " cabaret " show in the evening, already been mentioned, and of all the memories of that memorable date the one that lingers longest is the picture of the King and Queen departing from the festivities in the improvised " taxi," the King alternately honking on a Klaxon horn purloined from one of the launches or working joyously at the wheels of the foremost invalid chair to propel it along the quarter-deck. He was ever ready to join in any " rag " that happened to be going, and—sure passport to the claim to youthfulness—the ward-room and the gun-room both adored him. He was, when away from the trammels of official functions and from the chances of publicity, a high-spirited boy, full of fun and imbued with mischief.

Even ashore, there were times when he gave full rein to these qualities. One of the Press photographers at Christchurch attracted the King's attention by reason first of his long white beard, and secondly by his always being just too late to work in the picture he wanted. He was always there but never quite there, and though he must have been the oldest Press photographer in the world, he laboured most assiduously at his job. It is to be feared that the King teased him a little by allowing him to get the camera trained and then moving aside so that the photographer had to work round to a new position. At last the King relented and posed long enough for his pursuer to get a good picture. "Then," commented the King plaintively, "I'm hanged if he did not get his beard all tangled up in the shutter, so that I must have come out surrounded by a thicket of hair." Another photographic incident of the tour also brought out the King's mischief-loving fun. At one of the South Island towns the bouquet prepared for the Queen, who was then back in Wellington with tonsilitis, found its way into the hands of Mr. P. K. Hodgson, who wandered about the grounds looking most disconsolate and obviously wondering what to do with such an unaccustomed burden. An enterprising photographer snapped him and the resultant picture showing "Pat" as a younger, lovelier Bunthorne appeared in Wellington's leading pictorial. The first the King heard about it was a telephone message from the Queen, who had by then left the town, that the photograph was not on any account to be lost. A few days later the paper came to hand and the picture was an instantaneous success. The King gloried in it. He had the blushing photographer up at the earliest opportunity to congratulate him on the "best picture he had ever seen anywhere," and a few days later he showed he had not forgotten the episode when, at another town, he was handed a bouquet, ordered by the authorities under the assumption that the Queen was to be present. He

PROCLAIMED

FIRST BIRTHDAY AS KING GEORGE VI

looked quickly towards the group of pressmen who had shared in the fun of the previous photograph and with a Satanic wink handed the bouquet to Mr. Hodgson. But even a Press photographer was not quick enough for Mr. Hodgson this time. The bouquet was out of his hands and back in its box before a camera could be trained or a shutter clicked. When he heard that they had not been again successful the King's disappointment was manifest.

At Dunedin the King was taken to a museum where relics of the first settlers were preserved. Among these relics was an adaptation of a barrel-organ sent out for Church services. Its repertoire was therefore entirely of hymn tunes—and not too many of these—but the King insisted not only on playing the weird contraption with every appearance of happiness, but also that the members of his staff should do so too, until someone dropped a penny as a hint that the audience would like the musician to move on. Several times during the long railway journeys, when the train stopped at wayside stations and the usual crowd thronged round the Royal saloon, the King, a slim figure in tweeds, would slip out of the train from a carriage further forward, stroll down the platform, and join in cheering himself as though he was one of the local residents. Coming nearer home, no one who saw him will ever forget his perfect delight at the costers' ball when he took full control as M.C. of the lancers and taught his party how that half-forgotten measure should be danced. Or later, when, roaring with laughter at the spectacle of Lord Lonsdale being roundly kissed by an enthusiastic costeress (if that be the correct term), he found himself caught round the neck and treated in exactly the same way to his mingled embarrassment and amusement.

Let this book end as it began—on the note of home. For of all the characteristics which stamp him most of all as an Englishman, the love of home, of his wife, and of his children, mark the King out for the admiration and affection of every fellow Briton. That he is happy, very happy, in his married life is patent to everybody who comes into contact with them. At a dinner not so long ago he took occasion to censure mildly the bachelors present for that they still preserved their foolish illusions about the blessedness of the single state. "Go thou, and follow my example," was his adjuration to them. His married happiness was completed by the arrival of his two daughters, and his only reluctance about going away from London is the thought that he may have to leave "the babies" behind. That was the wrench when he and his Queen set out on their world tour, and the six months' absence was only mitigated by the daily receipt ashore and afloat of radio and cable messages as to the progress and health of their daughter. He has confessed that of all the hours of the day that he loves best it is that intimate time at tea, when the Princesses come down and the four of them are just father, mother, and daughters for a blissful hour or two. Rumour has it that he is an indulgent parent, but he has at times to administer rebukes and does it in the traditional style. Only a short while ago the Princess Elizabeth rose from the wrong side of the bed and absolutely and emphatically refused to have her teeth cleaned. The King had at length to be summoned to exercise his authority. He found the Princess sitting up in bed, her little mouth firmly closed, and her baby face grimly set. She had come to the conclusion that continued teeth brushing was a bore and she meant to put up with it no longer. On one side of the bed stood one nurse with a toothbrush all ready prepared ; on the other, another nurse with a tumbler of water. Not all the arguments or the persuasions of her father could move her. She was adamant. " At last," the King says, " a brilliant idea struck me. I said, ' Elizabeth, how does father do his voice exercises ? ' " Taken off her guard, the baby lips opened to the " Ah " sound, in went the toothbrush, and the battle was over, a triumph of strategy over violence.

More than that, the word " Home " to him, as to all true Englishmen, connotes more than the atmosphere of cities and of town houses. He and his Queen assuredly converted 145 Piccadilly into a house that one felt as though it were " lived in " the moment one entered its portals. To them it was, however, an abiding place for work and ceremony. Their true home, the home of their hearts, lay in the country, or as far in the country as could be achieved by a member of the Royal Family burdened with the many responsibilities that beset them. So it was, that first White Lodge in Richmond Park and then, later, the Royal Lodge, Windsor, under the loving care of the King and Queen took on the gracious aspect of an English country house—surely no more beautiful living-place can be found in all the world. The King himself is an enthusiastic gardener, knows much about flowers, and garden planning is one of his many hobbies. He and his Queen find their truest happiness in the peace and quiet of its surroundings with their two children revelling in the freedom of the grounds and devoting themselves to all the country occupations which can be theirs without fear of interruption or intrusion. With his accession, the King's interests in country life and country pursuits will be much enlarged, and his happiness thereby increased. During the life of King George V he had taken over a good part of the management of the Royal estates at Balmoral and Sandringham, and had busied himself in the interests of the farmers and their welfare, no less than he did in the interests and the welfare of industrial workers. King Edward VIII was not fond of the country, not particularly at any rate, and when he ascended the Throne the activities of both Balmoral and Sandringham suffered a change. Most of the staff at Sandringham went, pensioned or to other work, a large area was leased to tenant farmers, and generally extensive alterations and economies were planned or executed.

Now Balmoral and Sandringham are to return to their ancient glory. It has been officially stated that the King will see that they are carried on in the same way as during the reign of King George V, and it will be certain that the King will, as his father did before him, regard them both, as his home, and be able to say as King George did at his first Christmas broadcast : " I am speaking from my home and from my heart." In fact, in all things which endeared King George to the nation as a family home-loving Englishman, the new King will preserve the high traditions of his father, to be helped and encouraged thereto by the Queen and the young Princesses, whose character, moulded by their father and their mother, leans ever towards the same affections, the same surroundings as those of their parents.

Readers of the King's speeches continually find in them a line, a phrase, sometimes a word that is almost a self-revelation. In this regard the following quotations from a speech made by him come very appositely. He was addressing a Welfare of Youth conference at Croydon, and he chose as his text from the summary of the programme the heading " Recruiting and Preparation of Voluntary Leaders." After expressing his opinion that there was never a time in the world's history when real leaders were more urgently needed to grapple with the new questions and new problems that are continually arising, he went on to offer to his hearers his ideas as to the qualities required in a leader.

" To my mind he must possess three great qualities : personality, sympathy, and above all idealism. The man who wins the trust and confidence of his fellow-men so that they will follow him anywhere is the man who can combine in himself these three virtues. I do not think I need speak to you about personality; you all know what I mean by that. Of sympathy I will just say this: its keynote is personal contact and understanding. If you want to lead you must be able to understand and share the joys and troubles of those whom you are trying to help. You must look at things from their point of view as well as your own. . . .

" The third quality of the leader I have mentioned is idealism. Nobody can lead unless he has the gift of vision and the desire in his soul to leave things in the world a little better than he found them. He will strive for something which may appear unattainable but which he believes in his heart can one day be reached, if not by him, by his successors if he can help to pave the way. . . .

" If the youth of the Empire is to grow up healthy and happy, ' Service ' must be our watchword."

PERSONALITY, SYMPATHY, IDEALISM, SERVICE—
in those four words are epitomised the
pillars of the King's character.

INDEX

A

Alexandra, Queen, 16, 194
Analy, Lady, 80
" Anzac Day " in Melbourne, 178
Arkwright, Rev. E. H., 22
Ashburton, lambs at, 165
Australian tour, 132 *et seq.*
  speeches at Melbourne, 75, 180; at Canberra, 75
  the healthy child, 96
  farm schools at Pinjarra, 100
  children's farewell in Sydney, 103
  Labour leaders' tribute, 127
  importance of visit, 168
  democratic army, 168, 172, 178, 186
  arrival in Sydney, 169
  aboriginal displays, 176
  " Anzac " day in Melbourne, 178
  Federal banquet in Melbourne, 179
  Melbourne University " rag," 182

  ceremonial at Canberra, 184
  presents of livestock, 187

B

Baganda, the, 85
Baldwin, Rt. Hon. Stanley, 205
Bath Club, 13
Batterbee, Sir Harry, 132
Bay of Islands fishing, 152
Bennett, Sergeant, 161
" Bill, Mrs.," 10
Blue Nile Dam at Sennar, 92
" Bogus " Duke of York, 48
Boys' Welfare Society, 98, 109
Bowes-Lyon family, 53, 54
Bricka, Madame, 10
Brooke, Rear-Admiral Basil, 80
Brooks, Norman, 226
Bruce, Rt. Hon. Stanley M., 180
Buist, Lieut.-Com. Colin, 80, 133, 158
Butiaba, 89

247

INDEX

C

Camden Park, N.S.W., 124

Cameron, Pte., 13

Canberra :
the Federal capital, 169
ceremonial at, 184, 185
notable military review, 186

Cancer Campaign Presidency, 198

Canterbury, Archbishop of, 207

Carnegie Trust, 106

Cavan, Earl of, 132, 136, 139, 158, 183
Lady, 132, 158

Charlton, Matthew, 127, 173, 180

Christchurch (N.Z.) :
"a night out," 76
the "Bolshie" Mayor, 126
the Press photographer, 239

Collingwood, H.M.S., 26
at Jutland, 31 *et seq.*

Colon, 141

Colville, Admiral Sir Stanley, 26, 36

Corroboree in Queensland, 176

Coryndon, Sir Robert, 81, 84

Cotton in Sudan, 92

Crossing the line, 80, 143

Cumberland cruise, 24

D

Daudi Chwa, H. H., 86

David, M. S., 12

Dawson of Penn, Lord, 37

Derfflinger, the, 33

Dessau, Mdlle, 12

Duke of York, the "Bogus," 48

"Duke of York's Camp," 110, 213

Dukedom of York, 47 *et seq.*

E

East African Tour, 81 *et seq.*
arrival at Mombasa, 81
journey to Nairobi, 82
rhino and lioness shot, 82, 83
hunting in Kenya, 83
welcome at Entebbe and Kampala, 86, 87
to Lake Albert and the Nile, 89
through the Sudan, 91
Nubian review, 92
Sennar Dam, 92
varied experiences, 93

Edinburgh visit, 194, 195

Edward VII, 11, 16

INDEX

INDEX

visit to *Collingwood* at wedding, 60

Jubilee Trust Fund, 105

Memorial Fund, 106

kava drinking in Fiji, 148

death, 200

illness in 1928, 211

Germany visited, 192

Gilmour, the Hon. Mrs. Little, 133

Girl Guide's good deed, 171

Glamis Castle, 54, 55, 195

Great Hanish Island, 189; (a stalk), 232

Greig, Wing Commander Sir Louis, 44, 225

Grey, Zane, 153

H

Hakas, 156

Hansell, H. P., 12, 16, 18, 224

Henry, Prince, Duke of Gloucester, 43, 79, 211

Hewett, Sir Stanley, 37

Hinriksen, Mr. 194

Hodges, Frank, 118

Hodgson, P. K., 132, 240

Holland, H. E., 125

Hua, M., 12

Hunting, 15, 228

Hyde, Rev. Robert R., 113, 128

I

Industrial Welfare Society, 97, 113, 128

Ingram, Mrs., 225

Inverness, Earl of, 49

J

Jamaica, visit, 140

James II, Duke of York, 58

Jinjja, 84

" Johnston, Mr.," 28

Jones, J. Walter, 14

Jutland, 31 *et seq.*

K

" Kabaka," Uganda, 85

Kampala, 87

Khartoum, 92

King, H.M., George VI :
   birthday, 10
   education and early days, 10 *et seq.*
   squash rackets, 14
   to Osborne and Dartmouth, 18 *et seq.*
   Cumberland cruise, 23 *et seq.*
   gazetted to *Collingwood*, 26
   operation for appendicitis, 30

INDEX

INDEX

INDEX

INDEX

Hutchinson's

IMPORTANT NEW BOOKS FOR THE SPRING OF
1937

※※※※※※※※※

BIOGRAPHY & AUTOBIOGRAPHY
Memoirs

These two volumes of "Memoirs" are more than an autobiography. They are an indispensable authority on the origins and rise to power of the Labour movement in Great Britain, written by one of the few remaining leaders who has been in the fight from the beginning and who has never turned traitor to those who placed him in authority. Rightly or wrongly he has stood by his guns.

The author's father could neither read nor write, and earned 24s. a week. When ten years old the Home Secretary of later years was working in a mill as a piecer, dodging the looms, running barefoot over oily floors, and earning 10s. a week, which went to help feed his six brothers and sisters. The future Food Controller often went hungry. He tells the story of "Piecer" Clynes's first public speech to discontented mill-hands, of his meeting with Mary Harper, a fellow worker and later his comrade through life.

In 1906 Clynes faces a Parliamentary election campaign in Manchester, later becoming Vice-Chairman of the I.L.P. During the War he was appointed Food Controller and tells how "I had a tape-machine recording only the sinking of food-ships. . . . It was ticking away intermittently hour after hour . . . every ship lost meant yet another reshuffle to avoid starvation." In 1920-1 he was made Deputy Party Leader and Chairman of the Labour Party. Then, with Labour, Clynes becomes Lord Privy Seal and tells of his duties as liaison officer between the Premier and his principal Ministers. The ex-mill-hand now takes precedence before Dukes of the United Kingdom, and the great triumph of the son of an illiterate worker becoming Home Secretary is at hand.

To be published Autumn 1937.
Two volumes. 16 illustrations. Large Demy. 18s. each
by
THE RT. HON. J. R. CLYNES, M.P.

The Success of the Autumn Publishing Season
ARTHUR JAMES BALFOUR
First Earl of Balfour, K.G., O.M., F.R.S.
by his niece BLANCHE E. C. DUGDALE
(Mrs. Edgar Dugdale)
Vol. I. 1848-1906, Vol. II. 1906-1930. Each 18/- illustrated

All prices in this list are provisional and subject to alteration.

Reza Shah

Reza Shah, the Persian Peter the Great of today, must be comparatively unknown to English readers, but his story makes fascinating reading in spite of its obscurity. The author depicts the amazing feudal chaos of old Persia ; Reza's coup ; the farcical Constitution ; the crushing of feudalism, and Reza's enormous achievements on the scale of Alexander the Great.

Large Demy. About 20 *illustrations.* 18s.

by
MOHAMMED ESSAD-BEY

The Best of Me

Basil Maine is well known as an essayist, critic, novelist, and orator. In 1933 reviewers throughout Europe and America were unanimous in acclaiming his biography of Sir Edward Elgar as a "brilliant achievement". More recently his biography of His Majesty King Edward achieved a wide success. He has written brilliantly of the many personalities he has met and the interesting life he has led. *Large Demy.* 16 *illustrations.* 18s.

by
BASIL MAINE
Author of *Our Ambassador King*

The Romantic Life of Maurice Chevalier

This is essentially a sympathetic study and as such will appeal tremendously to thousands of fans. From a very early age and in his many curious jobs Maurice was always wanting to sing and dance, and in this charming story of his life a very vivid picture is presented of the vicissitudes through which he passed, and, later, of the glamorous life that became his.

Crown 8vo. 16 *illustrations.* 6s.

by
WILLIAM BOYER

My Ups and Downs

The title for Theodore Christy's autobiography is particularly apt, for, in the opinion of Field-Marshal Sir Evelyn Wood, there was no better man over the fences. Besides being Master of the Essex Stag-hounds, the author was also a great steeplechase rider and had many successes at Hunt point-to-point meetings. During the war he did splendid work supplying the Army with horses from Essex. A great sportsman and known to all the sporting world, Theodore Christy has written the most fascinating and delightful book, full of good stories and reflecting a witty and refreshing personality.

Large Demy. 16 *illustrations.* 18s.

by
THEODORE CHRISTY

Swinnerton : An Autobiography

In 1917 Frank Swinnerton became known all over the world with the publication of "Nocturne", which has been translated into every European language except Spanish. His list of novels is imposing ; he is well known as a critic and as an expert on the publishing trade, in which he has enjoyed a wide experience. His life and his books radiate a sane and balanced philosophy which, indeed, is the keynote of one of the most entertaining of literary autobiographies. *Demy. About 8 illustrations. About 10s. 6d.*

by
FRANK SWINNERTON
Author of *The Georgian House* (42nd thous.), *Elizabeth* (15th thous.), etc.

An Autobiography

Mr. W. B. Maxwell is a son of the famous Victorian novelist M. E. Braddon, and although reared in the literary atmosphere of her home, it was not for a good many years after growing up that he became an author himself.

Success came to him rapidly when he did make a start. His first three books, "The Ragged Messenger", "Vivien", "The Guarded Flame", one after another gave him a wide circle of readers, and established his reputation as a writer of serious purpose and strong power. But before this happened he had enjoyed the largest possible experiences of the world. He had been everywhere, seen everything, and known everybody. He was a hunting man, an artist, a traveller ; also a London club man.

With the War he became a soldier—an infantryman ; the maker of innumerable friends on the Western Front. Since then he has been Chairman of the Society of Authors, Chairman of the National Book Council, a member of the Council of the Royal Society of Literature, and an attendant at many other committees.

Those literary abilities which have made W. B. Maxwell one of the most important novelists today have perhaps never been better displayed than in this remarkable autobiography. *Large Demy. About 8 illustrations. 18s.*

by
W. B. MAXWELL
Author of *Himself and Mr. Raikes* (10th thous.), *We Forget Because We Must* (61st thous.), etc.

Buffets and Rewards
A MUSICIAN'S REMINISCENCES

Weingartner is, of course, one of the greatest conductors and composers of our time and amongst lovers of music has admirers all over the world. In his book he paints vivid portraits of some of the outstanding figures in the sphere of music. He knew both Wagner and Liszt intimately, and was a friend of Brahms. He has conducted in all the great capitals of the world, and gives us individual impressions of Rome, Venice, Paris, New York, Athens, and Moscow. *Large Demy. 17 illustrations. 18s.*

by
FELIX WEINGARTNER

A Century of Buckingham Palace

This fascinating story of Buckingham Palace, published some years ago, has been thoroughly revised and brought up to date. Recent photographs and details of the Royal household as it is today have been included.

Illustrated. 3s. 6d.

by
BRUCE GRAEME
Author of *The Story of St. James's Palace*, etc.

The Story of Windsor Castle

Bruce Graeme, who has written such widely praised books on Buckingham Palace and St. James's Palace, has now turned his attention to another Royal household. The result is a most interesting and picturesque account of England's most famous castle. Large Demy. Illustrated. 18s.

by
BRUCE GRAEME
Author of *The Story of Buckingham Palace*, etc.

The Countess from Iowa

Born in Hamburg, Iowa, the author of this book soon manifested a desire for the stage. Her beauty and talent—Huneker, famous dramatic critic, called her "The Elizabeth Farren of the American stage"—soon brought her a position in the well-known Palmer Stock Company.

Inevitably what the stage had was wanted by many others, and a German nobleman, Baron Guido von Nimptsch, married Miss Bouton and took her to Germany, where she moved in Court circles and captivated that society as easily as she had won stage audiences.

Later a divorce took place and the author married Count Nostitz, one of the richest of the Russian aristocracy. Petersburg society welcomed the Countess, who brought not only dignity but vitality and humour to her prominent position. Large Demy. 15 illustrations. About 15s.

by
COUNTESS NOSTITZ, LILIE DE FERNANDEZ-AZABAL

My Melodious Memories

Herman Finck, renowned wit and British composer, has been known and loved by the musical and stage worlds in England for forty years. He has played in many theatres, conducted before kings, and has known many celebrities of the age. He writes brilliantly, and with a sharp wit, of music, writers, clubs, hotels, and, of course, the stage. He has hundreds of amusing stories about hundreds of people, and the celebrities in his pages include the late King, King Edward, Pavlova, Sir Thomas Beecham, Sir Harry Preston, Sir James Barrie, A. P. Herbert, and a host of others.

Large Demy. 47 illustrations. 18s.

by
HERMAN FINCK

Dreyfus: His Life and Letters

This remarkable biography which throws so much new light on the life and trial of Dreyfus is divided into two parts. The first, which is by his son, is an account of the case up to Dreyfus's release from Devil's Island and his second condemnation. It contains a most important selection of letters from Dreyfus to his wife (and vice-versa) and to Dreyfus from various celebrities.

The second part is the pathetic and tragic story of the case from the second condemnation at Rennes in 1899 to his final acquittal in 1906, and is written by Dreyfus himself.

To read the authentic words of father and son in this amazing case is a moving experience, and the fact that the book clears up a number of doubtful issues makes it all the more interesting. *Large Demy. About* 16 *illustrations.* 18s.

by

PIERRE DREYFUS

❧

Autobiography

It is no exaggeration to say that S. P. B. Mais must have brought home the beauties of the English countryside to thousands of people. His books are the stories, one might almost say the diaries, of his travels over the country, whose joys few people can express more happily. His autobiography is a volume that will thus appeal to thousands, representing, as it does, the life-story of a man to whom the pleasures and beauties of the English countryside mean so much. *Large Demy. About* 16 *illustrations.* 18s.

by

S. P. B. MAIS

Author of *England's Pleasance, England's Character*

❧

A. E. Housman

A PERSONAL RECORD

Few people enjoyed any intimate friendship with Professor Housman, one of the greatest of classical scholars and a poet secure of lasting fame.

The author of "A Shropshire Lad" and "Last Poems" was popularly believed to have been an unapproachable recluse who lived in a lonely world of his own. This was the legend about him. How far was it true? Mr. Grant Richards, who published "A Shropshire Lad", and "Last Poems", and knew Professor Housman intimately for many years and travelled with him at home and abroad, answers the question in this book. It is a human and intimate account of the author's long association with a man who was only known to most people as the author of "A Shropshire Lad".

Demy. With a frontispiece. 12s. 6d.

by

GRANT RICHARDS

A History of Lloyd's

*O*ne *of the most brilliant critics of our day, gifted not only with rare critical acumen but also with a witty and pungent pen, Mr. Straus's excursion into a fascinating subject is an event of importance. To the ordinary man Lloyd's is a synonym for efficiency, but the reader is here taken far afield and is shown how from the humblest beginnings in a London coffee-house, this great company, linking land and sea in a world-wide net, has become a household word from John o' Groats to the Horn. The authorities at Lloyd's are putting all their archives at Mr. Straus's disposal, with the result that his history will be a full and detailed one with much interesting new material and with a clear explanation of exactly how Lloyd's works today.*

Large Demy. About 20 illustrations. About 18s.

by

RALPH STRAUS

Pauline Bonaparte

*F*rom *the age of sixteen, and possibly earlier, Pauline Bonaparte's whole life was taken up with the "seizing of hearts". A "gold-digger" of the eighteenth and nineteenth centuries, she was beautiful but never sentimental, which was perhaps the secret of her many amorous successes. Joachim Kühn has brilliantly re-created a vivid and colourful life about which little has been written.* *Large Demy. 13 illustrations. 18s.*

by

JOACHIM KÜHN

Anne of Austria : The Infanta Queen

*T*his *romantic biography tells the story of Anne of Austria during the first years of her marriage to Louis XIII of France, when, to distinguish her from Marie de Medici, the Queen Mother, she was always known as the Infanta Queen.*

Young, radiantly lovely, spoilt by her father, Philip III of Spain, Anne found her position in the Louvre, with its intrigues and cabals, almost intolerable. Her dawning love for her young husband was thrown back on itself by his coldness and indifference, and, bored and restless, she became petulant, frivolous, and vain, interesting herself only in the care of her beauty, in dress, and foolish flirtations.

The book ends with her meeting with Mazarin, and her realization of the greatest love in her life. *Large Demy. 16 illustrations. 18s.*

by

MERIEL BUCHANAN

"Old Q.'s" Daughter

Everybody who has heard of the famous Wallace Art Collection will be interested in Bernard Falk's new biographical study, " 'Old Q.'s' Daughter". Here, for the first time, is told the amazing history of the strange family to whom the nation owes the wonderful treasures to be seen at Hertford House. No small part of Mr. Falk's achievement has been to solve the multitude of riddles arising out of the disputed parentage and behaviour of the different characters. Who was the mysterious lady suggested by the title? In what sense was another member of the family (the second Marchioness of Hertford) the mistress of the Prince Regent, afterwards George IV?

Who was the father of Lord Henry Seymour (brother of the fourth Marquis of Hertford) about whom Paris of the 'forties and 'fifties raved? Was he the famous "Lord Steyne", the seducer of Becky Sharp in "Vanity Fair" (incidentally described by Mr. Falk in one remarkable chapter as "The Caliph of Regent's Park"), or was he Junot, Napoleon's famous general, or Montrond, friend and bugbear of Talleyrand?

Last but not least, who were the parents of Sir Richard Wallace, who gives his name to the famous Collection? Was the fourth Marquis of Hertford his half-brother or his father? In any case, who was Sir Richard's mother? Was she "Old Q.'s" daughter, as suggested by the "Dictionary of National Biography"? Mr. Falk has been specially privileged to search the archives of the Wallace Collection, and he is indebted to many of our Peers for hitherto unpublished letters throwing light on the obscure history of a family which, at one time, aspired even to the throne itself.

Large Demy. Frontispiece in colour, 34 illustrations. 18s.

by

BERNARD FALK

Author of He Laughed in Fleet Street, The Naked Lady, Rachel the Immortal

❧

IN PREPARATION

Five Years Dead

by

BERNARD FALK

A sequel to He Laughed in Fleet Street

❧

Cyrano de Bergerac

Mr. Humbert Wolfe has made a brilliant and original film version of incidents in the life of that immortal character Cyrano de Bergerac.

Mr. Wolfe's scenario is based upon Edward Rostand's play "Cyrano de Bergerac", which took Paris by storm when it was produced.

The scenario, the work of one of our leading poets and critics, marks an entirely new departure in film technique.

Mr. Wolfe has written a long and provocative introduction to the book which is certain to be the subject of considerable discussion.

Demy. About 8 illustrations. 10s. 6d. net

by

HUMBERT WOLFE

Forty Thousand Against the Arctic

H. P. Smolka, *the well-known journalist, whose recent articles in "The Times" on Arctic Siberia have aroused such widespread interest, has now written a most important and extraordinary book. Last summer he started his journey by ice-breaker and aeroplane to Northern Asia and the islands in the Polar Sea.*

During the last four years the Russian Government has embarked on the great scheme of exploiting the vast natural resources of Northern Siberia, establishing a sea passage round the Arctic coast of Asia, and a short cut from Europe to America in the form of a Trans-Arctic air line. There are probably few people who were aware of these developments before Mr. Smolka's recent journey and the subsequent publication of his articles.

Large Demy. About 70 illustrations. 18s.

by

H. P. SMOLKA

❦

Revisiting My Pygmy Hosts

Translated by GERALD GRIFFIN

In his two previous books Paul Schebesta has shown a deep insight into pygmy customs and ways of life. In this fascinating new book the author continues, in more intensive form, his investigations into pygmy culture.

Large Demy. About 50 illustrations. 18s.

by

PAUL SCHEBESTA

Author of *Among Congo Pygmies, My Pygmy and Negro Hosts*

❦

The Whalers

Unfortunately we are not able to announce the translation into English of a book by Alexandre Dumas. Nevertheless the impress of that great writer is on this book, and it is interesting to discover just where his influence changed Dr. Maynard's pages.

The book represents the diary of a French surgeon on whalers in New Zealand waters during several voyages from 1837 to about 1846. Dr. Maynard, a man of great culture and knowledge, tells in full detail and with any number of human touches the story of the lives of whalers and the killing of whales. Whether describing the natives and their customs, the superstitions of his shipmates, or the dangers faced and endured, Dr. Maynard is always interesting.

Crown 8vo. 8s. 6d.

by

DR. FELIX MAYNARD

Edited by ALEXANDRE DUMAS

Introduction and Notes by JOHANNES C. ANDERSEN, Chief Librarian, Alexander Turnbull Library, Wellington, New Zealand. *The translation by* F. W. REED.

TRAVEL, ADVENTURE & SPORT

An Authentic Account of the Voyage of the "Girl Pat"

*D*uring the early summer of 1936 the whole world was amazed and gasped at the daring of Skipper Orsborne and his crew. The story presented an amazing epic of sheer adventure which will go down in history as a great Saga of the Sea.

Sensation follows sensation in this extraordinary story in which the Skipper tells how, with only a sixpenny atlas for chart, and a match-stick for sextant, he and his crew sailed across the Atlantic.

The tale of how they bluffed an agent to secure repairs and fuel and even handsome tips for themselves, how they ran aground and starved, played the mandoline with sharks as an audience, is a stupendous one unparalleled in its sheer daring and gallant pluck. Their adventures are legion, but there is laughter mingled with the anguish of these stirring pages.

Demy. *About 16 illustrations.* *About* 10s. 6d.
by
SKIPPER ORSBORNE AND HIS CREW

❈

An African Travel Book

*M*r. Patrick Balfour is no ordinary traveller, for, as "Society Racket" proved, he has a profound knowledge of human nature and is yet able to write racily about it. His ability to write amusingly and intelligently will be once again proved with this new African book.

Demy. *About 20 illustrations.* 12s. 6d.
by
PATRICK BALFOUR
Author of *Society Racket, Grand Tour*

❈

A Book on the Australian Test Tour

*H*ere is no ordinary book telling the secret of So-and-so's bowling or a dry commentary of day-by-day cricket in Australia, but a book with more general interest, and written from the picturesque and social, rather than the technical, aspect. *Crown 8vo.* *About 16 illustrations.* 6s.

by
BRUCE HARRIS

❈

Flight Across Continents

*T*he author, a German, was put in prison for writing articles about Jewish persecution. He was released, but his passport and papers were taken from him. This extraordinary book describes his amazing adventures and experiences in escaping from Germany and travelling to England.

Demy. 10s. 6d.
by
WILLI MELCHERT

Air Over Eden

*T*here are many books of travel, but this is an exceptional one. The aim of the authors has been to write a modern air book about Iraq, a country richer in historical associations than almost any other country in the world. The authors describe the country as seen from the air, and they also give a fascinating outline of its history, which began with two people in the Garden of Eden.

The book is at once a bird's-eye view in the very real modern sense of the term and a remarkably vivid survey of 5000 years of history.

Large Demy. 69 *illustrations.* 18s.

by

"H W" and SIDNEY HAY

✣

Milestones in the Air

*A*s a complete vade-mecum on aviation this book can have no rivals, but it is written by a journalist, in fact the "Evening Standard" Aviation Correspondent, and the popular element has consequently not been overlooked. Mr. Courtenay has many amusing and amazing stories to tell of his wide experience in modern flying. He tells the story of an air tour with Sir Alan Cobham. Having been adviser to Amy Mollison his book contains much that is new concerning her flights and rise to fame. There are new scoops, tales of his own flying experiences, the author's feelings on crashing, plans for the Atlantic air route, the future of air travel, and a host of new and witty stories about famous airmen and airwomen, in this fascinating and informative book.

Demy. *About* 16 *illustrations.* 12s. 6d.

by

WILLIAM COURTENAY

✣

Whirlpools on the Danube

*"W*hirlpools on the Danube" is an account of a journey made through some of the Danube countries of Europe during the summer of 1936.

The author of that excellent book, "German Journey", left London and travelled fairly rapidly to Southern Germany and across the Austrian frontier, to the Tyrol, and sets down his impressions of this popular district of Austria. Czechoslovakia, the next country visited, is the newest European nation, and her problems are new. From there, Subcarpathian Russia, the author travelled to Budapest and the Hungarian countryside. From there the author returned to London, via Transylvania, and in the last chapter of this fascinating book sums up his impressions and thoughts of four months' travelling.

Large Demy. 48 *illustrations.* 18s.

by

CHRISTOPHER SIDGWICK

Author of *German Journey*

England's Character

In this book of Mr. Mais's recent wanderings round the countryside he has not only described fresh places, he has talked with and listened to all sorts of Englishmen, from gamekeepers to poachers, parsons to tramps, bus-conductors to auctioneers. He traces a Roman road over the fields in Shropshire; he attends a sheep fair in Sussex; cattle markets in Wiltshire and Devon; he watches salmon being netted on the Taw; travels through the night by bus to Monmouth, and by day up the Great North Road to Darlington; he pays a visit to the hop-pickers in Kent, and passes the "Queen Mary" on her maiden voyage home.

He describes a morning's cub-hunting at daybreak and a day in chase of the otter, the last cricket match of the season on the village green, and the life of London's suburbs. By this means he has traced a pattern of England's character that shows how little, in spite of superficial changes, the character of the countryside or of its people has changed.

Crown 8vo.   15 illustrations.   7s. 6d.

by

S. P. B. MAIS

Author of *England's Pleasance*

Australian Fantasy

Taking as his inspiration a gallery of notable photographs, Mr. Dudley Glass weaves around them an Australian fantasy. Its lavishly illustrated pages conjure up a bushland of strange plant and animal life; paint a scenic wonderland of blue mountains and golden beaches and sun-burnt pastures; shows from a new angle a young country at work and at play. Begin the story among Stone Age aboriginals and end a cavalcade of progress in ultra-modern cities. A colourful Australia is captured in this series of admirable camera-studies accompanied by their complementary pen-pictures.

Size 11 by 8 ins.   Beautifully illustrated.   7s. 6d.

by

DUDLEY GLASS

Author of *The Spanish Goldfish*, *The Book About the British Empire*, etc.

Changing Horizons

Major Foran started his travels abroad nearly forty years ago, long before the vogue of the "luxury cruises". His wanderings have taken him far and wide on the Seven Seas, both on and off the beaten tracks. Seldom has the same ground been covered more than once. His progress was unhurried, so unusual opportunities came in his path for seeing places and things which are not generally in a traveller's itinerary.

Traveller, explorer, and novelist, Major Foran knows well how to invest his travels with a vividness and clarity of expression that enable the reader to become an eye-witness of the many fascinating places which he visited.

Large Demy.   63 illustrations.   18s.

by

W. ROBERT FORAN

Author of *Malayan Symphony*, *A Cuckoo in Kenya*, etc.

Crowning the King

"Coronation Day is going to be a day to be remembered for a lifetime. For on that day King George will ride in state to Westminster to be crowned the undoubted King of his realm."

Thus the opening words to this fascinating and extraordinarily interesting book in which the author tells the history of coronation and kingship from ancient times. He has sought to give an account of the coronation ceremonies which shall be clear, accurate, and readable. It has been his aim to present the knowledge of historians in a form which young people can read and follow. He also sketches the life of the King and the circumstances leading up to the Coronation. It is a knowledgeable book, written for the purpose of explaining the significance and details of the Coronation to the countless thousands whose interest it will be. *Crown quarto. Four colour plates and about twenty black-and-white illustrations. 5s.*

by

LEWIS BROAD

❧

An A B C Guide to the Coronation

This book is indeed a happy thought of Lewis Broad's, for this year everyone will want information on such an important subject. It has been concisely drawn up, and on account of its size and price is a book that should be in everyone's pocket. *Crown 8vo. About 20 illustrations. 6d.*

by

LEWIS BROAD

❧

The Coronation of the Kings of England

In "This England" Mr. Shears showed himself to be a man with a very deep knowledge of English customs and places. His book was a masterpiece of patient research and careful selection of material. In his hands the stories of the Kings of England become not only interesting, but also lose that film of unreality with which countless educational works have endowed them.

About 3s. 6d.

by

W. S. SHEARS
Author of *This England*

❧

Rex, The Coronation Lion

James Riddell's new book of the Adventures of Rex, who comes down from his place in front of St. Martins-in-the-Field for the Coronation, will amuse grown-ups and children. His ancient enemy, the Unicorn, is also in Town on Coronation Day, and the fun is fast and furious. *Illustrated. 3s. 6d.*

by

JAMES RIDDELL
Author of *Let's be Gay, Let's be Absurd*

Collected Essays and Observations

As one of the most prominent personalities in England today, Lord Hewart, of course, needs no introduction. A very full life has accorded him little time for the gentler art of writing, but the essays which he has chosen to publish have been widely read and appreciated, and this, his latest volume, will appeal to many readers. Demy. With a frontispiece. 10s. 6d.

by
LORD HEWART
(*Lord Chief Justice of England*)

❈

Physic and Fancy

There are many wise and amusing statements in this physician's note-book. The author has jotted down random thoughts and statements on all manner of things, and uses, often very skilfully, medical facts to illustrate the points he wishes to make.
It is indeed a book of parts, for mingled with sound medical advice is a rare and sane philosophy of life. Readable, interesting, and bearing comparison, in its form, with the famous "Notebooks of Samuel Butler", it forms a curiously unusual and inspiring piece of work. Large crown 8vo. 6s.

by
CHRISTOPHER HOWARD

❈

Company Finance

Famous as a novelist, as a journalist, and as one of the most expert of writers on financial matters, Collin Brooks contributes one of the soundest and most comprehensive volumes on Company Finance yet written.
Crown 8vo. 3s. 6d.

by
COLLIN BROOKS

❈

Claims of the Lesser Creeds

The editor of this volume is a well-known expert and an author of great repute. His collection of the various Creeds of Great Britain will be a somewhat unique one supplying a great need.
The claims in this comprehensive and illuminating volume are set out quite impartially, and readers can judge for themselves of their value.
Demy. About 31 illustrations. 18s.

DUFF SESAME, B.D. (*Edited by*)

The Year Illustrated—1936 in Pictures

One of the most remarkable book values ever offered. The breathless panorama of many world events pictured in a beautifully produced volume. And eminent authorities discuss in illuminating little articles the significance of such all-important happenings in the march of world history.

Over 300 unique photographs on fine art paper. 96 pp. 14 by 10 ins. 3s. 6d.

PAUL POPPER (*Edited by*)

❦

Woman Adrift

In this new book Mrs. Cecil Chesterton has taken the subject of "Woman Adrift" and has once again written a most appealing and knowledgeable volume. Demy. About 8 illustrations. 10s. 6d.

by
MRS. CECIL CHESTERTON
Author of *In Darkest London, Women of the Underworld*, etc.

❦

I Am Going to Have a Baby

It would be difficult to imagine a title that sums up its subject more aptly than this. It is, however, necessary to point out the sane and sensible way in which the subject has been treated. It is a plain and straightforward account of invaluable use to every prospective mother. It contains advice on matters which, if overlooked, may be disastrous.

Crown 8vo. About 16 illustrations. 6s.

by
MARTHA BLOUNT

❦

Bloomers

The success of the "Howler" books has been enormous and has resulted in the author receiving any number of new errors, dropped bricks, faux pas, and other curious misrepresentations of our language. Here are one or two examples of this gorgeous collection :

From Cincinnati : "Here lies Jane Smith, wife of Thomas Smith, marble cutter. This monument was erected by her husband as a tribute to her memory and a specimen of his work. Monuments of the same style 350 dollars."

"They gave Wellington a glorious funeral. It took six men to carry the beer."

"C.I.D. means Copper in Disguise."

This book, presenting the rich humour of "howlers", will cheer you at any time.

Crown 8vo. Illustrated. 1s. 6d.

by
CECIL HUNT
Author of *Howlers, Fun With the Famous*, etc.

Autobiography

"Daily Telegraph"

"There isn't a dead, a dull, a false, or a pretentious sentence."—SIR JOHN SQUIRE.   *Illustrated.* 10s. 6d.

by

G. K. CHESTERTON

❊

Arthur James Balfour

"Evening Standard"

". . . Vivid descriptions of public affairs, striking sketches of public men— a veritable cavalcade of interesting and dramatic episodes and personalities."— SIR IAN MALCOLM.   *Illustrated. Two vols.* 18s. each.

by

MRS. EDGAR DUGDALE

❊

Memoirs

"Sunday Times"

"An eminently readable account of people and places that have made history during the past fifty years."   *Illustrated.* 16s.

by

H.R.H. THE INFANTA EULALIA

❊

Sixty Years Ago and After

"Daily Mail"

"It is to be hoped that his extremely entertaining book is only a first instalment of his reminiscences."   *Illustrated.* 18s.

by

SIR MAX PEMBERTON

❊

Walter Long and His Times

"Daily Telegraph"

". . . Many sidelights on politics during the last 60 years revealed for the first time."   *Illustrated.* 18s.

by

SIR CHARLES PETRIE

Sylvia of Sarawak

"Morning Post"

"An easy-going, full, human, and very entertaining book."   Illustrated.   18s.

by

H.H. THE RANEE OF SARAWAK

❈

Leaves from My Unwritten Diary

"Birmingham Mail"

"Sir Harry must have met every sportsman of note in his time, and his stories, with their wealth of humour and detail, are indeed a tribute to this remarkable little man's memory."   Illustrated.   12s. 6d.

by

SIR HARRY PRESTON

❈

Ilonka Speaks of Hungary

"Sunday Times"

"A lively and amusing companion."

"Daily Telegraph"

"Stimulating and entertaining."   Illustrated.   10s. 6d.

by

JOHN BROPHY

❈

German Journey

"John o' London"

"He has reported his observations with fairness, some vividness, and an honest absence of pretension."   Illustrated.   18s.

by

CHRISTOPHER SIDGWICK